LILY CHIN'S

Knitting
*tips&
tricks

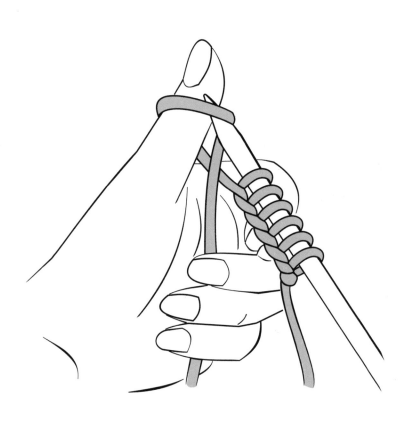

LILY CHIN'S

Knitting *tips& tricks

SHORTCUTS and **TECHNIQUES**
every knitter should know

by Lily M. Chin

ILLUSTRATIONS BY KARA GOTT WARNER

POTTER
CRAFT

NEW YORK

Copyright © 2009 by Lily M. Chin

Published in the United States by Potter Craft, an
imprint of the Crown Publishing Group, a division of
Random House, Inc., New York.

www.crownpublishing.com
wwww.pottercraft.com

POTTER CRAFT and colophon is a registered
trademark of Random House, Inc.

Library of Congress Cataloging-in-Publication Data

Lily Chin's Knitting Tips & Tricks:
Shortcuts and Techniques Every Knitter
Should Know / by Lily M. Chin.

p. cm. Includes bibliographical references and index.

ISBN 978-0-307-46105-6

1. Knitting. I. Title. II. Title: Knitting tips & tricks.

TT820.C484926 2009

746.43'2—dc22

2009021443

Printed in the United States

DESIGN BY CHALKLEY CALDERWOOD
ILLUSTRATIONS ON PAGES, 15, 16, 18, 23, 24, 30, 60, 71–85, 89, 91,
94, 117, 118, 123, 124, 157, 160, 180, 185 BY FRANCES SOOHOO.
ALL OTHER ILLUSTRATIONS BY KARA GOTT WARNER.

10 9 8 7 6 5 4 3 2

First Edition

This book is dedicated to the memories of my
recently deceased **mother** and **sister.**
They both nurtured my love of craft from an
early age and both left me way too soon.

Contents

8 * Introduction

1

Needles and Yarn

14 * Needles

19 * Yarns

2

The Basics

36 * Before you Begin

40 * Knitting Basics

3

Getting Started

60 * Making a Swatch

82 * Adjusting Garment Lengths

87 * Working with Coned Yarns

90 * A Better Cast-On— Using Mathematics

97 * Casting On in Pattern

99 * Crocheted Cast-On

102 * Chained Provisional Cast-On

4

As You Work

112 * Joining New Yarn

117 * Working with Ribbon yarn

119 * Working Stripes

121 * Intarsia Color Changes

122 * Knitting in Pictures

125 * Decreases

132 * Increases

137 * Fixing Mistakes

5

Finishing

148 * Binding Off

156 * Blocking

162 * Seaming

172 * Joining as You Go

178 * Setting in Drop-Shoulder Sleeves

184 * Spacing Buttons Evenly

186 * Making Buttonholes

195 * Weaving in Ends

200 * The Lowdown from Lily

202 * Abbreviations 203 * Resources 204 * Bibliography 204 * Acknowledgments 205 * Index

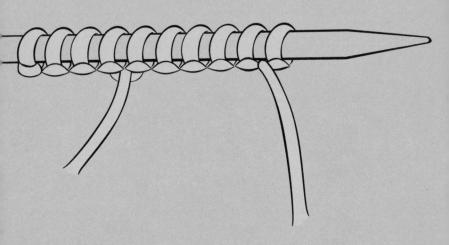

Introduction

I envision this book as one of my most
popular classes
brought to the printed page.

I've taught a tips-and-techniques class

for more than a decade, and it still
always sells out—
just about instantly. As a result, countless other
knitters
have voiced their frustration at not having the benefit of
knowledge.

I have had many, many students who have been knitting for years ask, "Why didn't I think of that?".
I've also had relatively new knitters in my classes,
and I'd like to think I have gotten them started
on the right foot, so to speak.

Why You Need
This Book

THERE ARE TONS OF STANDARD TECHNIQUE BOOKS on the market right now. What you hold in your hands is a book full of things that I've come up with over the years that solve **my personal knitting problems** and bugaboos. As a result, you most likely will not find them in the standard technique books. Famous knitting guru Elizabeth Zimmermann called this "unvention." That's when you come up with something on your own, but you know you can't possibly be the first one to think of it. Although a lot of these techniques, tips, and tricks are not common knowledge, many have become more popular, I'm sure, as a result of the classes that I have taught almost every month since 1994. Word gets around. Thus, some things may be familiar to you, but I guarantee **many are eye-openers**.

We all love knitting, yet there are certain aspects of the process with which we're not overly fond. (Can we say "weave in the ends"?) **I've come up with simple ways to make the annoying parts easier;** hopefully they will make your knitting life a lot more enjoyable and trouble free. You will find that these techniques can be applied to any of the projects you are currently working on, so you can use these tips and tricks almost immediately.

In the book, I cover things chronologically; the tips and techniques are presented in the order of your knitting process. One of the first things you do when you begin to knit is to cast on (chapter 2). One of the first things you make before you begin a project is the sample swatch (chapter 3), and so on.

I'm sure that, over the years, you may have come up with your own tips and tricks—things that you've unvented. Maybe one day we can all compare notes and begin a massive database. Until then, enjoy!

In This Chapter

14 Needles
14 Needle Types
16 Needle Materials
17 Needle Sizes
19 Yarns
19 Yarn Fibers
22 Yarn Texture
23 Yarn Thickness
25 European and Australian Standards
27 Unraveling the Secrets of Cone Yarn

Needles and Yarn

The stuff you work with can make or break your whole knitting experience. **Use good tools** and get yarn that's not only right for your project but also that you enjoy working with. You have many choices, so try out a few different kinds of yarn and needles to see what works for you.

Needles

· ·

We live in an era of bountiful knitting options, and the tools we use have never been more varied and diverse. We can choose needles made from many materials, in certain styles, and even with different types of points.

Needle Types

Other than for the sake of collecting or for bragging rights, why do you need so many needles? And what do you want to look for in a needle? The first thing you want to consider is the project you will be making. Some kinds of needles are traditionally better suited for one type of project rather than another.

Straight needles

These traditional needles, which come in several lengths, are generally used for flat, back-and-forth knitting of pieces of limited width.

Circular needles

These needles joined by a thin cable are normally used for circular or seamless knitting, though they may be used for flat or back-and-forth work as well, especially for wider pieces. They are available in different lengths.

Double-pointed needles

These needles, also available in several lengths, are used for smaller circular knitting.

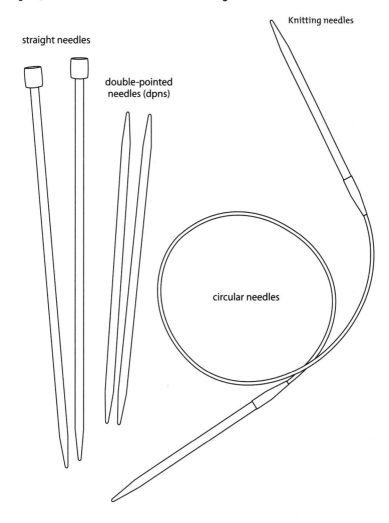

straight needles

double-pointed needles (dpns)

Knitting needles

circular needles

Choosing your needles is a fiercely personal thing. If you prefer to make your socks on small circular needles or two circulars rather than on double-pointed needles, go for it. Some people prefer straight needles for all projects; they always use long straights— tucking the needles under their armpits— and can't maneuver circulars at all. Just make sure that the needles you choose are adaptable to the pattern you are using.

Needle Materials

It used to be that needles were made from metal, bone, or wood; ivory and tortoiseshell were the occasional "exotic." Now, needles can be made from a whole host of materials from plastic to unusual hardwoods to eco- logically friendly bamboo, from the humble aluminum to nickel-plated and brass. You can even get needles made of glass, as well as those that glow with an internal light source!

Needle tips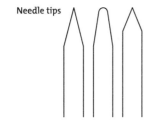

A word on needle tips. In addition to dif ferent needle types, there are different shapes of tips; that is, there are distinct shapes to the tip or the pointy part of a nee- dle—some are rounder and others sharper.

I've heard many knitters say they like the rounder tips because they don't split the yarns as much. Others prefer the pointy ends because they're easier to insert into the stitches. I encourage you to try them all, in different materials, to find what works best for you. I personally favor the pointy circulars, but that's due to my own knitting style.

Needle Sizes

Needles come in a large range of sizes. In the United States, they are numbered: the

Knitting Needle Conversion

U.S. Size	Metric Size	UK/Canadian Size
0	2	14
1	2.25	13
2	2.75	12
	3	11
3	3.25	10
4	3.5	
5	3.75	9
6	4	8
7	4.5	7
8	5	6
9	5.5	5
10	6	4
10½	6.5	3
	7	2
	7.5	1
11	8	0
13	9	00
15	10	000

higher the number, the larger the needle. In most of the rest of the world, however, needles are measured in millimeters. Be aware that there also exists an older British system where the larger the number, the smaller the needle. The previous table illustrates the sizes and their equivalents.

HOW TO FIND OUT THE SIZE OF A NEEDLE. If you have a needle with no indication of its size, an extremely useful device is the gauge check, a flat rectangle made of plastic or metal with holes of different sizes. You just stick the needle through a hole. Alas, some needle sizes may fall through the cracks: They don't fit properly in any of the holes. I've known some very particular knitters who've used jewelers' fine calipers to determine needle diameters. More and more, needles have their sizes imprinted on them. Some fun acrylic ones are even color coded for easy identification.

A needle gauge

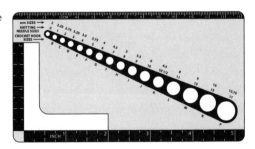

Yarns
• •

As with needles, we are luckier than ever in the many choices we have for yarn today. In addition to a vast array of colors, yarn comes in different weights, textures, and fiber combinations.

Yarn Fibers

Yarns are made of many different materials, often referred to as content. There's the traditional wool and cotton (natural fibers) and acrylic (man-made). There are also exotic animal fibers from the alpaca, the angora rabbit, the angora goat (mohair), the cashmere goat, and even possum from New Zealand and the occasional hand-spun dog hair! Qiviut comes from the downy underwool of the Arctic musk ox, quite rare and expensive. There's been a return of vicuña, an even more uncommon and expensive yarn from a relative of the South American alpaca and llama. In my stash, I have such rarities as yarn from fox, chinchilla, mink, yak, and buffalo.

Blending different fibers can impart the best of all worlds. A bit of acrylic can lighten up and make stretchy the inelastic cotton. Acrylic can also make wool machine washable and/or dryable. Wool introduced into an exotic can make it more affordable.

Yarn Content

Type	Origin	Characteristics/Comments
Wool	Sheep (including Merino, Shetland, Icelandic)	Versatile, warm, and very elastic. Feel and appearance can vary with breed.
Silk	Silkworm (a cocoon secretion)	Slick and sleek. Both warm and cool with no elasticity.
Alpaca	Alpaca (from South America)	Warm with medium elasticity.
Mohair	Angora goat	Hairy or fuzzy. Warm with limited elasticity.
Angora	Angora rabbit	Very hairy. Very warm with limited elasticity.
Camel Hair	Camel	Warm with medium elasticity.
Llama	Llama (cousin to the alpaca; originally from South America)	Warm with medium elasticity.
Cashmere	Goat	Very warm and luxurious. Medium elasticity.
Yak	Yak	Very rare. Warm and limited elasticity.
Qiviut	Arctic musk ox	Similar to cashmere but warmer.
Guanaco	Guanaco (a threatened relative of the llama from South America)	Very rare and expensive. Warm with limited elasticity.
Vicuña	Vicuña (an endangered relative of the llama from South America)	Very rare and expensive. Warm with limited elasticity.

Type	Origin	Characteristics/Comments
Cotton	Cotton plant	Cool. Can be left matte in its natural state or made shiny through mercerization. No elasticity.
Linen	Flax plant	Stiff, but softens upon washing. Cool with no elasticity.
Rayon/Tencel	Reconstituted tree pulp	Cool and slinky with no elasticity.
Bamboo	Reconstituted bamboo pulp	Smooth and cool with no elasticity.
Ramie	Reconstituted pulp of ramie plant	Combines the properties of cotton and linen. Cool with no elasticity.
Hemp	Hemp plant	Linenlike. No elasticity.
Soy	Soybean by-product	Cool. No elasticity.
Banana Fiber/Corn	Reconstituted fiber (from fruit tree bark or corn plant)	Cool with no elasticity.
Milk Protein	Milk casein (milk protein)	Cool with no elasticity.
Chitin	Reconstituted shrimp and crab shells	Cool with no elasticity.
Metallics/Metals	Metals	Slinky or scratchy, depending on the metal used and construction method. Shiny and cool, some can be sculpted.

Yarn Texture

Fuzzy, smooth, nubby, tufted—yarn comes in all textures. A unique construction or way the yarn is created results in interesting yarns known as novelty yarns. A bouclé has bubbly loops, a brushed yarn is hairy, a tape yarn looks like ribbon. Combine construction with content and you have an abundance of combinations such as a cashmere tape or a mohair bouclé or a brushed acrylic, and many more. See the yarn chart below for more information.

Yarn Construction

Type	Description
Bouclé	From French word meaning "curl." Loopy. Often hard to see stitches.
Chenille	Fuzzy, plush. Beware of tendency to worm (or loop out), and to bias and shed.
Eyelash	Hairy, fuzzy. Often hard to see stitches.
Microfiber	Very fine thicknesses achieved mostly with synthetic fibers.
Ribbon	Flat tape. Can be knitted or woven.
Slubs, Nubby, Thick and Thin	Uneven thickness of yarn throughout. Sometimes lumps or bumps appear after thin areas.

flat tape or ribbon

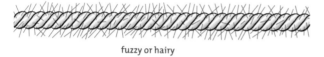

fuzzy or hairy

bouclé

● **TIP** MORE (FUZZ) THAN MEETS THE EYE
**Some yarns may seem small but will work
up to a larger stitch (and gauge) than you
would think. Yarns that have fuzz, such as
mohair, or yarn that takes up "airspace,"
such as bouclé, can be deceiving.**

Yarn Thickness

In the United States, the mills have traditionally spun certain standard thicknesses
for the commercial hand-knit market.
These weights are known as fingering,
sport, worsted, and bulky.

Traditionally, finer yarns are used for
socks, underwear, and baby items. Since
there are more stitches required, these
items, though small, may take the same
amount of time to knit as a larger item

(such as an adult sweater) in a medium- or heavyweight yarn. The advantage of using finer-weight yarns is that the fabric produced is thinner and drapes nicely. Bulkier yarns are usually used in jackets and outerwear. Though the resulting fabric is generally chunkier and does not drape as well, projects are usually quicker to finish.

For more on yarn weights and thicknesses, I refer you to the website of the Craft Yarn Council of America (CYCA) and its yarn standards (http://yarnstandards.com/weight.html). Not only does this site contain useful charts with needle sizes and yarn weights, but other pages give you great information on standard abbreviations, yarn label information for the care of the project, size and garment measurements, and other guidelines.

Yarn thickness

A good place to start with yarn weight is to look at the information on the yarn label. There is usually a recommended gauge size, such as 4 stitches per inch (2.5cm) or 6 stitches per inch (2.5cm), as well as a suggested needle size. Remember that these are just recommendations and suggestions. Feel free to use the needle size that will get the recommended gauge. Conversely, if you feel the fabric of your swatch is just fine on the needles that you've chosen, which are different from those suggested on the label, feel free to deviate.

European and Australian Standards

Imported yarn often uses different weight standards. In the United Kingdom and throughout most of Europe, you will get names such as four-ply, double-knitting (or DK), Aran, and chunky. To confound things even further, Australia classifies its thicknesses as four-ply, six-ply, eight-ply, and so on, even though there may not be that many strands or plies in that yarn. See the chart on page 26 for the Australian yarn equivalents. Even if the names are different, the recommended gauge is a great clue to the yarn weights. Again, refer to the standard yarn weights chart from the Craft Yarn Council for help in sorting out yarn thicknesses.

Australian Yarn

Australian Yarn	Gauge per 10cm (4 inches)	Needle Size	U.S. Weight	CYCA Category
3-ply	32 stitches/40 rows	3.25mm (U.S. 3)	Fingering	0 Lace
4-ply	28 stitches/36 rows	3.25mm (U.S. 3)	Sock, fingering, baby	1 Superfine
5-ply	26 stitches	3.75mm (U.S. 5)	Sport, baby	2 Fine
8-ply	22 stitches	4mm (U.S. 6)	DK	3 Light
10-ply	20 stitches	4.5mm (U.S. 7)	Light worsted	3 Light
12-ply	17–18 stitches	5–5.5mm (U.S. 8–9)	Worsted	4 Medium
14-ply	14–15 stitches	6–6.5mm (U.S. 10–10.5)	Chunky	5 Bulky

● **TIP** WRAPS PER INCH

Another way of classifying yarn weights is a system used primarily by weavers that is called wraps per inch or wpi. Wrap yarn around a pencil or ruler and count how many wraps there are in one inch. The heavier the yarn, the fewer wraps; the thinner the yarn, the more wraps. Here is a table of wraps per inch for U.S. yarn weights.

Wraps

Yarn (U.S.)	Wraps Per Inch
Fingering	17–18 wpi
Sport	15–16 wpi
DK	14 wpi
Worsted	12–13 wpi
Aran	10–11 wpi
Bulky	8–9 wpi
Super Bulky	6–7 wpi

Unraveling the Secrets of Cone Yarn

Some industrial-type yarns that are usually found on cones use a mysterious series of numbers such as 5/2 or 2/28 These counts indicate yarn thickness and the number of plies. It is an international standard that the manufacturing industry uses, mostly for yarns used for weaving and for machine knitting. There are actually a few different systems, but the worsted system for wool and acrylic fibers is one of the most typical.

The Worsted System

In this system the first number is the number of plies. So, for example, 1/5.5 means it's a single-ply or one-strand yarn. The second number is based on length per fixed weight, which in this case is 1 pound (454g). The number of yards per pound will vary, but for whatever reason, it's measured by how many 560-yard (512m) hanks there are in this pound.

Thus, the higher the number, the thinner the yarn. For example, it takes a whopping 2,000 yards (1,829m) of a sportweight yarn to weigh a pound, but only 800 yards (732m) of a worsted weight. In a single-ply, the sport weight would be 1/3.5 (it takes three-and-a-half 560-yard hanks to get 2,000 yards in a pound), and the worsted would be 1/1.4 (it takes one and four-tenths of a 560-yard hank to get 800 yards in a pound).

So let's say it takes five-and-a-half hanks of 560 yards each to weigh a pound, and it is a single-ply. That would be 1/5.5. Here's the math to figure out what weight of yarn it is: Five and a half times 560 equals 3,080 yards (2,816m) per pound. A pound is equal to 454 grams, and 3,080 yards divided by 454 equals 6.78 yards (6.2m) per gram. This means a 50-gram ball has 339 yards (310m); that would be similar to a British four-ply weight (between sport weight and fingering weight).

A 2/28 means there are two plies, and each of the plies is so thin that it takes twenty-eight hanks at 560 yards (512m) each to achieve a pound—actually 15,680 yards (14,338m) total.

The Cotton System

The cotton system is similar to the worsted system; they just invert the numbers and use hanks of 840 yards (768m). Thus, a 5/2 yarn has two plies and requires five hanks of 840 yards (768m) to equal a pound.

The Denier System

The denier system is used for continuous-filament silk spinning. So when nylon (or artificial silk) came on the scene, this was also measured in a denier count, which is a measurement of the weight per fixed length. It is the opposite of the worsted system. Instead of the weight being fixed, the yardage is fixed. The fixed unit length is 9,000 meters (9,843 yards), so in this system you want to know how much 9,000 meters of a given yarn weighs. Obviously, 9,000 meters of a thick yarn would weigh more than 9,000 meters of a thin one.

Unlike the worsted system—the higher the number, the finer the yarn—in this system it's the lower the number, the finer the yarn. So a filament of 2 denier is twice as thick as a filament of only 1 denier. One denier means the yarn weighs just 1 gram per 9,000 meters. It is so thin that anything thinner than this is classified as a microfiber, which has a general thickness of one-sixtieth that of a human hair!

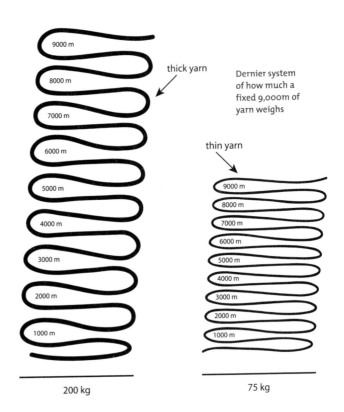

thick yarn

Dernier system of how much a fixed 9,000m of yarn weighs

thin yarn

9000 m
8000 m
7000 m
6000 m
5000 m
4000 m
3000 m
2000 m
1000 m

9000 m
8000 m
7000 m
6000 m
5000 m
4000 m
3000 m
2000 m
1000 m

200 kg

75 kg

The Tex System

The tex system was introduced as a universal system to replace all existing systems, but it has not been widely accepted. It is a measurement of the number of grams per 1 kilometer, or 1,000 meters, of yarn, not dissimilar to the denier system. In this system, a 50-gram ball of DK or light-worsted knitting yarn typically measures about 100 meters (109 yards). That means 1,000 meters would weigh 500 grams (1.1 pounds) so the yarn is 500 tex. The number of plies and the direction in which the plies are twisted together are also included in the designation. For example, on a label that reads "R 500 Tex / 4 S," *R* means resulting count or total count, and *4 S* means there are four plies twisted in a counterclockwise direction or S-twist (as opposed to a clockwise or Z-twist). However, each one of the four plies has a 125 tex since the four combined make up 500 tex (or R).

To summarize, here is a synopsis of the most common systems.

- **Bradford Worsted System:** The number of 560-yard (512m) hanks that weigh 1 pound (454g).
- **English Woolen System:** The number of 256-yard (243m) hanks that weigh 1 pound (454g).

- **English Cotton System:** The number of 840-yard (768m) hanks that weigh 1 pound (454g).
- **Continental Metric System:** The number of 1,000-meter or 1 kilometer (1,094-yard) hanks that will weigh 1,000 grams or 1 kilogram (35 ounces).
- **Denier System:** The weight in grams of 9,000 meters (9,843 yards).
- **Tex System:** The weight in grams of 1,000 meters (1,094 yards).

If all this seems confusing, just remember that worsted-weight yarn is 1,000 yards (917m) per pound, sport weight yarn is about 1,500–1,800 yards (1,375–1,651m) per pound, and fingering weight is around 2,000 yards (1,829m) per pound.

On the other hand, if this subject fascinates you, you can learn more with an online search for "yarn numbering system."

● **TIP** MATCHING NEEDLES TO YARNS

A big key to success in knitting is matching the appropriate needle type to yarn type. Not only do you want a proper needle size to use with the proper weight of yarn, but the type of needle you choose can make knitting with a particular yarn easier and more pleasant. For instance, when the yarn is slippery, such as a mercerized cotton or a slinky rayon, use a grabby needle type such as bamboo or wood or even some plastic varieties. Conversely, when the yarn is grabby, such as a matte chenille, try a slick type of needle, such as a nickel-plated one. If a yarn splits easily, go for a more blunt tip. If a yarn is thin, a pointier tip helps you work into the stitches much better. Sometimes, a luxury yarn such as angora might call for a luxury needle such as ebony just for the sheer decadence of it!

If you find yourself struggling with your project, a change of tools may be the answer. Another type of needle, even in the same size, can alter your gauge. Experiment with a few different ones. If you find that you can't seem to get gauge, try birch instead of aluminum, or plastic instead of bamboo. Needles can induce "moods" into your piece. Metal, cold to the touch, can cause some knitters to tense up. Wood, which is warmer to the touch, can relax other knitters. These factors can also affect your gauge.

2

In This Chapter

36 Before You Begin
36 Holding the Needles
38 Holding the Yarn
40 Knitting Basics
40 Casting On
47 The Orientation of a Stitch
48 The Knit Stitch
50 The Purl Stitch
52 Stitch Patterns
56 Binding Off

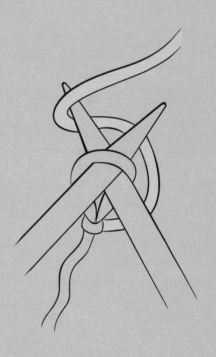

The Basics

This book addresses knitting right-handed. I often **encourage** left-handed beginners to try to knit right-handed because it will make following directions a lot easier later. **Knitting is, after all, a two-handed activity.** If you are left-handed, try each way of holding the needles to see which works best for you.

Before You Begin

Hold it right there! Hold it—the needles and the yarn, that is—in the most comfortable way for you so that knitting will be a pleasurable experience. Alas, ergonomics and effectiveness may not always be in sync; that is, the best way to produce a stitch may not feel comfortable for you at first. In order to get that next loop through that previous loop, you may feel as if you're going through contortions. Needless to say, that old adage about practice and perfect does ring true. If you do something often enough, it will feel more natural. If it doesn't, then try another approach to achieve the same results.

Holding the Needles

Fights break out among knitters on the proper way to hold the needle. Trust me, use whatever works for you. It is truly a matter of personal preference. There are two basic ways to hold the needles, referred to as English and Continental.

Holding English

In this method, probably used by the majority of knitters in the United States, the yarn is held in the right hand and is "thrown" around the needles. Many people refer to this method as throwing. Within this method, there are two ways to hold the needle. Some hold the right-hand needle like a knife, others hold it like a pencil. In Victorian times, the pencil hold was preferred, as it was deemed more ladylike and dainty.

I personally use the knife hold, as it gives me better control. I also find the knife hold easier on the hands and wrists—they do not have to make more contorted moves that can result in stress and pain. Again, try both to see which you like more.

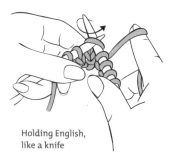

Holding English,
like a knife

Holding English,
like a pencil

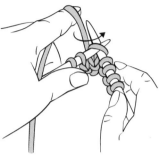

Holding
Continental

Holding Continental

The yarn is held in the left hand for Continental knitters—this type of action is similar to crochet in this respect. Crocheters may find the Continental hold more familiar and therefore easier. The yarn is "picked up" by the right needle, so many refer to this method as picking.

Holding the Yarn

Regardless of how you hold the needle, holding the yarn is by and large the same. The major difference is in which hand you hold it. The yarn should wind around the pinky finger first, then up and over the index finger. This gives some tension to the yarn, creating more control over your gauge. Some knitters twirl the yarn around the index finger for even more tension.

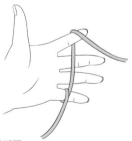

Holding the yarn

● **TIP** SMOOTHING OUT TOOLS

From time to time, needles can drag a bit, except for the more expensive nickel-plated needles, which are very slick. There are several ways to revitalize and smooth the surface of needles.

For years I've applied a bit of hand cream or lotion to coat the tips of my needles, which I then wipe with a tissue to remove the excess. This leaves a nice, slick residue. Every month, I wash the needles and reapply. Some people have advised using waxed paper to gloss over the needles, while others suggest rubbing the needles through the hair and scalp to pick up natural oils. I find the hand cream method longer lasting than the hair treatment, and I always have cream or lotion around, but I don't necessarily have waxed paper readily available. In a pinch when traveling, I've even used liquid soap from public restrooms!

If nicks or burrs develop on the needles, try smoothing them with an emery board or fine grit sandpaper, then apply the hand cream or lotion and the needle will be as good as new. I do this for almost all types of needles, from wood to aluminum to plastic.

Knitting Basics

• •

It is still infinitely fascinating to me how one can take a length of string and manipulate loops to create a piece of fabric or sculpture. And each loop is connected to the others both horizontally as well as vertically. The structure of knitting is not difficult to figure out, and if you study the way the loops are picked up, you will have a better understanding of the craft. Once you see how knitting is constructed, you will also see its unending possibilities.

Casting On

In the beginning, you have to get the first stitches onto the needle. This is called casting on. This lays down a foundation, much like masons do when working with brick. Each stitch is a unit going across the piece; this establishes the width of the piece. The more stitches there are, the wider the piece. Then you work stitches on top of these stitches, one at a time going across, and this is called a row. More rows of stitches are worked over these stitches to create the height of the piece, or the vertical dimension. There are many ways to cast on those first stitches. Here are three basic methods that have proven to be extremely versatile.

● **TIP** WHAT'S A SLIP KNOT?

This is a knot that is very helpful for casting on. It's also a knot that can be easily undone. Take your yarn and make a loop as shown. Now if you take your needle out and pull on the end, out it comes. You don't want to pull it out for the cast-on. The slip knot stays on the needle (neither too loosely nor too tightly).

A slip knot

Half-Hitch Cast-On

Also called the backward loop cast-on, this is the simplest cast-on and perhaps the one most of us learn as beginners. It is not very stable, however, because the stitches tend to spread farther and farther apart on the needle when you are working the first row, leaving a long strand between the stitches. That's not to say it isn't useful,

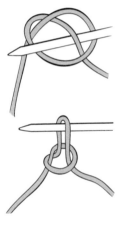

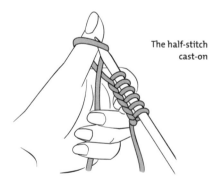

The half-stitch cast-on

especially when adding several stitches at the ends of your rows or for buttonholes.

As with most cast-ons, it begins with a slip knot. Hold the needle with the slip knot already on it (this counts as the first stitch) in the right hand and the yarn in the left hand. Hold the yarn overhand like a knife. *Free up your thumb. Have the thumb go up and over, then under the yarn, making a circle as you catch the yarn. The yarn is now looped over your thumb, making the backward loop. Insert the needle through the loop from left to right, or front to back, as shown and tighten the loop slightly (but not too tightly). This forms another stitch on the needle. Repeat from * until you have the required number of stitches.

Long-Tail Cast-On
This is one of the most elastic and stretchy cast-ons. It uses a length of yarn reeled off to provide a long tail, hence its name. There are two ways to make this cast-on; the "slingshot" is the most common. Some people choose to begin with a slip knot while others can do without. I start with a slip knot.

For the slingshot method, reel off some yarn, make a slip knot, and then place it onto the right-hand needle as the first stitch.

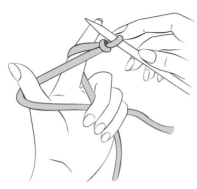

The slingshot
formation

With the left hand, grasp both the tail and
the working end of yarn about 2–3 inches
(5–7.5cm) from the needle in an overhand
position as if holding a knife. Free up the
thumb and the forefinger. Notice how the
last three fingers are holding the yarn now.
Insert the thumb and the forefinger
downward from above between the two
strands of yarn and splay them apart to
separate the strands. Now flip the wrist
backward and you have the classic slingshot
formation, with one strand forming a loop
over the thumb and the other strand making
a loop over the forefinger.

   *Insert the right-hand needle into the
loop around the thumb as if to knit: Pretend
the left thumb is like the left-hand needle
and insert the right-hand needle into the
thumb loop from front to back. "Scoop" the

The long tail cast-on

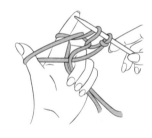

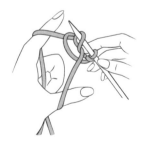

yarn on the index finger through the thumb loop as if it were ice cream; that is, bring the right-hand needle down onto the index-finger yarn from the back and pull it through the loop on the thumb. Now bend the thumb to drop the thumb loop and tighten the loop.

With some practice, you will drop only the thumb loop and tighten it as you maintain the slingshot formation. After bending the thumb to drop its loop, reinsert the thumb down from above between the two strands, spread it away from the index finger, and catch the same strand as before to get a new thumb loop. The loop on the index finger remains in place throughout. Now repeat from * until you have the required number of stitches.

The spreading action also serves to snug up the base of the stitch you just cast on. If you want any horizontal elasticity to your cast-on, leave a little slack between stitches. You may have read elsewhere that to get more slack you should use a larger needle, but that really doesn't help with this kind of cast-on. That's because it's the tension of the thumb yarn that snugs the stitches together. A larger needle only makes larger stitches; it doesn't have any effect on the tension of the thumb yarn.

LONG-TAIL CAST-ON USING THUMB LOOPS.
Another way of doing the long-tail cast-on is
with one strand of yarn in each hand. After
placing the slip knot onto the right-hand
needle, hold one strand in the left hand and
loop it onto the thumb as before. Insert the
needle into that thumb loop as if you have
just gone into a stitch to knit it. While keeping that loop on both the needle and your
thumb, use the right hand to wrap the other
strand of yarn around the needle as if to
knit, then lift the left-hand thumb-loop up
and off the needle, letting the thumb loop
drop off the thumb. Make a new thumb loop
for each stitch. The results of this method
are the same, but it may be easier for some
knitter to use separate hands.

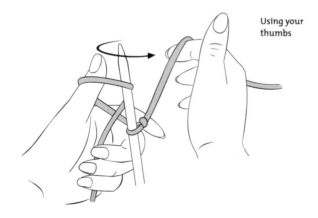

Using your
thumbs

Knitted Cast-On

I like starting rank beginners with this cast-on because it introduces the basic action of the knit stitch as they are casting on. Again, begin with a slip knot on the needle as your first stitch, but this time leave a tail of 4–6 inches (10–15cm) from the beginning of your yarn. Hold this needle in your left hand. *Insert the right-hand needle into the front, or right "leg," of the first stitch from front to back, holding the working yarn in back. Wrap the yarn around the right-hand needle by bringing the yarn underneath it, then come toward you and over the top of the needle. Pull on the yarn slightly for tension as you use the right-hand needle to draw this wrapped yarn back out through the stitch toward you. This creates a new loop on the right-hand needle. Transfer this new loop from the right-hand needle onto the left needle. Tighten the new stitch a bit but not too tightly. There are now two stitches on the left-hand needle. Repeat from * to create as many stitches as you need.

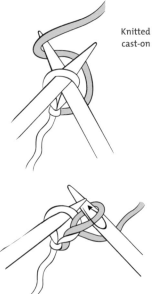

Knitted cast-on

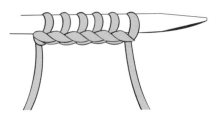

The Orientation of a Stitch

The loop of a knit stitch is almost like a
doughnut with the hole facing front. In order
to get this loop onto the barrel, or cylinder,
of a knitting needle, it has to turn sideways.
The direction of this sideways turn is very
specific and important. On the needle, the
right leg comes forward and is in front of the
needle, while the left leg moves to the back
behind the needle. Should the stitch loops
drop off the needle, remember to place them
back on this way. The right leg is also sometimes referred to as the leading leg, as it's
the closest to the needle tip and is the
leg into which the needle is inserted. The left
leg is sometimes called the trailing leg.

There are some knitters who deliberately
orient their stitches in the opposite direction,
which is not uncommon in the Continental
style of knitting. These knitters usually know
how to compensate for this by still knitting
and/or purling into the right leg of any
stitches that are now behind the needle, that

A stitch on
the needle

is, knitting/purling into the *back* loops of the stitches. These knitters are often referred to as Eastern uncrossed or Combination style knitters. However, for now we will deal with the more standard orientations.

The Knit Stitch

As I mentioned earlier, knitting is simply pulling a new loop through an existing loop, and the needles just facilitate this action. You can hold the needles and yarn any way you like as long as you produce that loop and get it through that old one sitting on the needle. (However, see page 37–38 for the standard needle-holding methods.)

To knit, hold the needle with the cast-on stitches in your left hand. *Insert the free right-hand needle into the front (or right leg) of the first stitch on the left-hand needle from front to back, holding the yarn in the back. Wrap the yarn around the right-hand needle underneath while coming toward you, then over the top while going away from you. Pull on the yarn slightly for tension as you use the right-hand needle to draw this wrapped yarn out through the loop toward you. This creates a new loop on the right-hand needle. Use the right-hand needle to pull the old stitch off the left needle. Repeat from * across all the stitches on the left-hand needle. This completes a row. Then just switch the needles of each hand—which is called turning your work—and begin again.

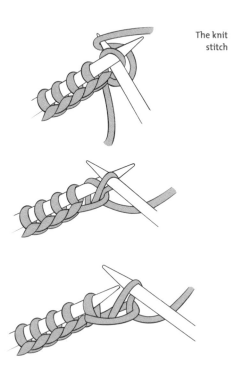

The knit stitch

The Purl Stitch

The purl stitch is just the back side of the knit stitch. Purl stitches are formed in a similar manner but with important differences. To begin, hold the needle with all the loops in your left hand, but start with the yarn held in front instead of in back as with the knit stitch. To purl, *insert the free right-hand needle into the front (or right leg) of the first stitch on the left-hand needle from back to front. Wrap the yarn, which is now in the front, around the right-hand needle over the top while going away from you, then underneath while coming toward you. Pull on the yarn slightly for tension as you use the right-hand needle to draw this wrapped yarn back out through the stitch as if you're pushing it away from you. This creates a new loop on the right-hand needle. Drop this first stitch from the left-hand needle. Because there is new yarn going through or atop this old stitch, it will not go anywhere when you drop it. Repeat from * across all the stitches on the left-hand needle. This completes a row. Then just switch the needles of each hand—turning your work—and begin again.

The purl
stitch

Stitch Patterns

By combining the basic knit and purl stitches in different ways, you can create an infinite number of patterns. Using stitches in certain ways produces different kinds of knit fabric.

Garter Stitch

Garter, or garter stitch, is made by working rows of the knit stitch only. Because the knit side of a row is smooth and the purl side is bumpy, this pattern has alternating ridges of bumpy and smooth on either side, making it reversible, and it lies flat with no curling. Think about this construction. When you knit, a purl shows up on the back side. Yet when you turn your work around to work the next row, the bumps face you. As you lay down new, smooth knits over these bumps, you're producing bumpy purls on the back side atop smooth knits on the back side. Make sense?

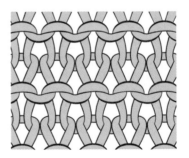

Garter stitch

Stockinette

Stockinette, or jersey stitch, is made by alternating a row of knit stitches with a row of purl stitches. This forms a smooth side, called stockinette, and a bumpy side, known as reverse stockinette, because, after completing a knit row and turning the work around, the bumps then face you. When you work this side as purls, it keeps the bumps on this side and the smooth stitches on the other side. Conversely, when the smooth knits face you, you're working more knits over these. Stockinette is one of the most common stitch patterns and is the foundation of many other types of knitting such as lace, cables, and colorwork. Unfortunately, this fabric does curl at all the edges. That's why other stitch patterns, such as noncurling garter stitch, often are worked as trims around stockinette.

Stockinette

Reverse stockinette

Alternating stitch types across the row, either knit or purl, is a bit more complex. It involves having to bring the yarn back and forth from back to front, since knits are created with the yarn in back and purls are formed with the yarn in front. When bringing the yarn from one side to the next, make sure the yarn goes *between* the needles and not over them so you do not get an extra loop on the needle that you could mistake for another stitch. If you do that, you'll wind up with extra stitches and gaping holes.

Ribbing

Ribbing is a classic example of these mixed stitch patterns. In ribbing, knit alternates with purl. Cast on an even number of stitches. Begin with a knit stitch, then bring the yarn to the front to form a purl stitch, * bring the yarn to the back to make a knit stitch, bring the yarn to the front to form a purl stitch; repeat from * to the end. Turn your work and work all subsequent rows the same. Notice how the knits fall above knits and the purls stack on top of one another as well. Ribbing forms a springy, stretchy fabric usually found at the edges of a garment. Ribbing lies flat and does not curl.

There are many rib variations. For instance, if you alternate 2 knits with 2 purls, the rib lines get wider; and a knit 3, purl 3 rib is even wider. The number of knits and purls don't always have to be equal. In the conventional knit 1, purl 2 rib, there is a one-to-two ratio of knit to purl stitches.

Seed Stitch

Seed stitch is much like ribbing, with knit 1 and purl 1 alternating across the row. The difference is that on subsequent rows, you knit over the purls and purl over the knits as you see them. "As they face you" or "as they present themselves" are two of the terms found in instructions. Seed stitch forms a knit fabric with nubby texture that also lies flat. To try it, cast on an odd number of stitches and work all rows the same as follows: knit 1, purl 1 across, knit the last stitch.

Seed stitch

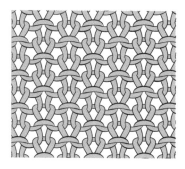

● **TIP** READING YOUR KNITTING

I strongly recommend investing in a stitch
dictionary to check out all the lovely and in-
triguing patterns. I also recommend learning
to recognize the stitch that's on your needle.
That way, you can visually see what stitch
needs to be worked next rather than have to
remember the pattern or sequence. This is
often referred to as "reading your knitting"
and is an exceptionally useful skill to develop.

Binding Off

At the end of your project, you will have to
get rid of all the stitch loops on the needle.
You can do this while knitting or purling or
working a combination of the stitches. Often,
instructions will say "bind off stitches in
pattern," that is, knit *or* purl them as
indicated in your particular stitch pattern
before binding them off. To begin, work the
first two stitches only. There are now two
stitches on the right-hand needle. With the
tip of the left-hand needle, lift the first
stitch on the right-hand needle up and over
the second one. You have now eliminated the
very first stitch, and one stitch remains on
the right-hand needle.

* Work another stitch so that there are two stitches on the right-hand needle again. With the tip of the left-hand needle, lift the first stitch on the right-hand needle up and over the second one. You have now eliminated another stitch, and one stitch remains on the right-hand needle. Repeat from * until only the last stitch remains on the right-hand needle. Clip the yarn leaving about 4 inches (10cm) of tail, bring the tail through this last loop, and pull to tighten. This is called fastening to end off.

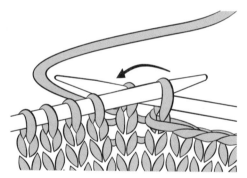

Binding off

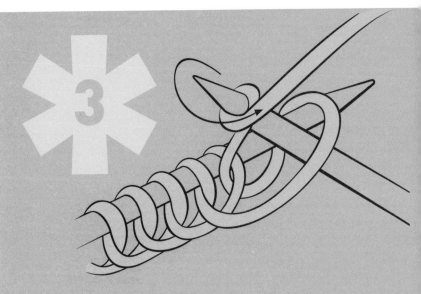

3

In This Chapter

60 **Making a Swatch**

60 What Is Gauge?

65 Washing and Blocking the Swatch

67 Measuring the Swatch

71 The Hung Gauge

74 Weighing In

75 Using Your Swatch to Estimate
Your Yarn Needs

80 Using Your Swatches

82 **Adjusting Garment Lengths**

87 **Working with Coned Yarns**

90 **A Better Cast-On—
Using Mathematics**

93 Yarn for Seaming

97 **Casting On in Pattern**

99 **Crocheted Cast-On**

102 **Chained Provisional Cast-On**

105 Crochet Chain Cast-On Variation

Getting Started

There are many **tips, hints, and tricks** here that will make your knitting experience more enjoyable; but the first—and the most important one—is to **make a swatch** before you begin knitting. You'll be amazed at how much information you can get from a swatch!

Making a Swatch

The *very* first thing you should make before you begin a project is the gauge swatch. Although it's not so important for items such as scarves or stoles or afghans that don't have to be an exact size, getting the correct gauge when knitting a garment is crucial if you want it to fit. If you're making a garment and refuse to swatch, all I can say is that you get what you deserve!

What Is Gauge?

And why is getting the gauge important? Gauge is the number of stitches and the number of rows it takes to get a certain measurement. That measurement is usually taken over a 4-inch (10cm) square, though many patterns talk about gauge in terms of one inch, such as "4 stitches per inch" or "5

Billiard balls and marbles

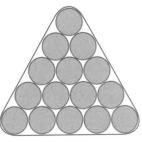

Billiard balls

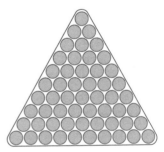

Marbles

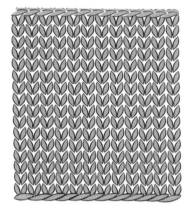

Swatch made with bulky yarn

Swatch made with fine yarn

rows per inch." If the size measurement of your stitches and your rows do not match that of the pattern, the piece you knit will not be the intended size.

I like to use the analogy of billiards. The first step before playing is to rack up the billiard balls, that is, place them into the triangular-shaped rack. There are fifteen fat billiard balls that fit into that rack. Now, what if you used marbles rather than billiard balls? How many marbles will fit into that same triangular rack? A whole lot more.

Instead of a triangular rack, let us imagine a square one that is 4 inches by 4 inches (10cm by 10cm). The number of stitches that fit into that square rack is the gauge. Heavy and bulky yarns are your billiard balls. The stitches are so big that you can only fit a small amount (like twelve) in there. The thinner and finer yarns are like the marbles. The stitches are smaller so you can fit a large amount, perhaps as many as forty-nine, in the square.

If your gauge is larger or looser than called for, that is, if you have fewer stitches and rows in a 4-inch (10cm) swatch than specified, the finished piece will be too big. Conversely, if your gauge is smaller or tighter than called for or you have more stitches and rows than required in a 4-inch (10cm) swatch, the finished piece will be too small.

Exactly how big should your swatch be? Almost all measurements are specified for a 4-inch (10cm) square. Since the edges do not lie flat, you want to make a swatch bigger than that. I like a 6-inch (15cm) square so I can make a 1-inch (2.5cm) border all around. If the gauge is given for a repeat of a stitch pattern, work either plain stitches on either side or work more of the pattern on each side. If the repeat is very large, work plain stitches. Always bind off the swatch before measuring. With knitting still on the needle, the stitches may stretch and distort too much for an accurate measurement.

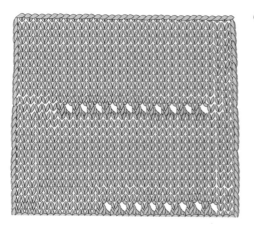

Coded swatch

● **TIP** ENCODE YOUR SWATCH

After making a gauge swatch, you may not always begin the project immediately. You may have gotten gauge the first time, but it does you little good if you've forgotten what needle size you used! Here's a way to remember the needle size. Like Madame Defarge in *A Tale of Two Cities*, you will encode it by making a hole, or eyelet, in the bottom of your swatch as many times as the number of your needle size.

To make an eyelet, yarn over (yo) and knit two stitches together (k2tog). The yarn over—wrapping the yarn around the needle in a knitwise fashion (as if you were going to knit)—creates an extra stitch, but the knit 2 together takes away one so that the stitch count remains the same. Later when you see eight eyelets or holes, you will know the swatch was worked on a size 8 needle. (By the way, this yarn over/hole technique is used to make eyelets when knitting lace.)

What about metric needle sizes? With a 2.25mm needle size, you could work two eyelet holes at one end of the swatch and another two at the other end. On the second row, work five holes at any one end. For a 2.75mm needle, work two eyelets at the beginning and seven at the end, then on a following row add five more eyelets above the seven. What to do with a U.S. size 10$\frac{1}{2}$ needle? I say work ten holes and a bobble (several stitches worked into one stitch). That bobble means something "extra."

Notice that on the sample swatch (page 63), there are two sets of holes, one at the bottom and one midway up. I didn't get the correct gauge the first time on size 8 needles (see the eight holes at the bottom) so I had to go to larger needles. If that happens to you, continue working on the same swatch. Why bother having to rip out and cast on all over again, and why add more wear and tear on your yarn? The eyelet holes will also let you know when you changed needle sizes.

I have to thank the craft of machine knitting for this tip. I (and many other machine knitters) have been using this trick forever; I just applied it to hand knitting. I strongly urge you to become familiar with other crafts. You can find lots of good things to adapt to knitting.

Washing and Blocking the Swatch

Do you think you'll ever launder your projects? Well, most of us plan to wash our knit items at some point. The golden rule of knitting is "Do unto the swatch what you will do to the project." How do you know if the red and white stripes will become a pink blur? How do you know that silk won't grow or that cotton won't shrink? The swatch will tell all, at least most of the time. You don't want any surprises. Measure the swatch and take note of its condition before and after washing to see if there are any changes. Some like a wet block, but I prefer the steam method (page 156).

Would you ever buy a car without taking it out for a test-drive first? Making a swatch is like test-driving your yarn. I frequently buy just one skein of a yarn before investing in all the yarn for a project. Will a particular cashmere pill? Will this yarn hold up under some wear and tear? I pin the swatch to the inside of one of my garments and wear it around or stuff it inside my purse. I call this the torture test. If it still looks good and not too worn, I will then go for the whole shebang. It's better to know sooner rather than later that my time and effort will be rewarded.

Sometimes a yarn label states "dry clean only." I know for a fact that many of these yarns can indeed be hand-washed. Manufacturers do this to minimize liability. They don't want mobs of angry knitters trying to sue them if the results are unsatisfactory. How do you know if the yarn can indeed be hand-washed? You guessed it: Wash the swatch. You'll find you can save yourself some costly dry-cleaning bills and be a friend to the environment while you're at it.

● TIP CONDITIONING YOUR WOOL YARN

If a wool yarn is rough and scratchy, put some hair conditioner or creme rinse into the wash. This will soften the fabric considerably. After all, what are woolens but animal hair, and animal hair will respond to conditioner just like your hair does.

Measuring the Swatch

Measure the stitches with a ruler or other straightedge or a gauge check, not a flexible tape measure, in a few places to get an average. Sometimes, if you're tense and stressed, the gauge is tighter. Conversely, if you're more relaxed and at ease, the gauge is looser, so taking a measurement over a few places and averaging it is best. If your swatch has more than just a small difference from one spot to the next, it will be safer to knit it again.

● **TIP** READING THE GAUGE

What if you have difficulty distinguishing the stitches in your swatch easily because your yarn is dark or highly textured or both, like black mohair? Here is a cheat: Have another smooth, contrasting color of the same yarn weight on hand. Cut two yarn strands of this contrasting color, about 8 inches (20.5cm) of each. Let's say the gauge is supposed to be twenty stitches and twenty-eight rows in a 4-inch (10cm) square. If you're making a 6-inch (15cm) square as recommended above, there should be thirty stitches across, with five stitches on either side of

Color block swatch

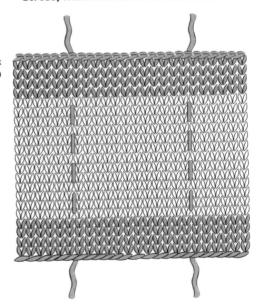

the twenty in the center 4 inches (10cm). There should be forty-two rows total.

Cast on the thirty stitches with the contrasting color yarn. Work a few rows with this contrasting yarn, then switch to the main working yarn. At this point, keep count very carefully of the number of rows worked in the main yarn. After completing the first row with the main yarn, work the first five stitches, place one of the contrasting strands to the left of the stitch just knit and work the next twenty stitches, then place the other contrasting strand to the left of the last stitch you made, and work the last five stitches. Continue in this manner, carrying the contrasting yarn upward between the stitches every third row or so, not every single row. After completing the prescribed twenty-eight rows, work a few rows in the contrasting yarn again and bind off. These strands of contrasting yarn almost look like basting threads, and you will be able to measure the distance between them to see how many inches these twenty stitches equal.

The contrasting rows you worked before and after the main yarn also will help you measure the length of your twenty-eight rows. You have a clearly defined rectangular block of color to mark off twenty stitches and twenty-eight rows. This method also takes a lot of the guesswork out of patterned stitches, such as seed stitch, and even more intricate ones. Just another hint I got from the world of machine knitting.

● **TIP** SEEING THE GAUGE

If the yarn is heavily textured, lumpy, fuzzy, or bumpy, you may not be able to see the stitches clearly enough to read the gauge. If you did not use the rectangular block method described above in your swatch, perhaps because you didn't have smooth, contrasting yarn in the same weight on hand, then you'll have to "see the light." Tape the swatch to a window on a sunny day. You should be able to see the light streaming through your stitches and be able to count the stitches and measure the gauge.

Even if you're not concerned about gauge, for example on a scarf, working with novelty yarns can often be problematic. That brown bouclé or that navy eyelash can make it difficult to find where to insert the needle. Use this same principal of backlighting your work by placing a lamp on the floor, which should make it easier to see the stitches. Some knitters place a light-colored towel or cloth on their laps for a similar effect.

I have a friend who is a doctor, and when she works the graveyard shift, she often tapes her swatches to an X-ray viewing machine. What a funny sight that must be.

The Hung Gauge

After making the swatch, most knitters lay it on a flat surface to measure it. If the project is a garment, you will now know how big this piece will be if you were to wear it while lying down in bed! There is a force in nature that Sir Isaac Newton talked about in the mid 1600s: It's called gravity. You can emulate the effect of gravity on the knitted fabric by hanging up the swatch. I use masking tape on a wall, but straight pins along a towel on the rack or pushpins on a corkboard will work equally well. Hanging the swatch creates a more accurate picture of what the fabric will measure when it "grows up," or in this case, grows down. Have you ever had clothes that literally grow on you? The length gets longer. Now, since there is a fixed amount of yarn in this swatch or in that sweater, something's gotta give. It stands to reason, then, that if it grows one way (lengthwise), it will compensate by shrinking the other way (widthwise). That cropped

The potential growth of a swatch

and boxy vest can become a skintight dress before the day is through. (If you plan to make a blanket or anything else that lies flat, this step is not necessary.)

Some fibers such as cotton, silk, and rayon are big culprits of this phenomenon. What do they have in common? They are all inelastic. They have no memory and will stretch out but not return to their former shape.

Some other factors will also influence growth. If you loosen up a gauge or use a needle size much larger than called for, this will compromise the structural integrity and can cause the knitted fabric to grow. And very heavy or thick fabrics tend to do this, too. A garment made with super bulky or dense yarn that weighs as much as 2 or 3 pounds can be pulled down by its own weight.

This vertically grown gauge is known as a hung gauge for obvious reasons. Let the swatch hang for a day before measuring. Take a "before" gauge measurement with the swatch lying flat. Compare it to the "after" hung gauge and note the difference. Your work may come off the needles one size, but after hanging it may become another size. When directions say to "block pieces to measurement," it means to let it grow to the hung gauge. You can force this in the wet blocking process by pinning it to size, but I prefer steam blocking. When directions say to "work until piece measures 12 inches (30.5cm) from beginning," if there is a difference between the hung gauge and the flat gauge, rather than work to that measure, work to the hung row gauge. To do that, figure out how many rows will be worked in 12 inches (30.5cm) before blocking and work to that number of rows rather than rely on the measurement. The nice thing is that once you've factored in the growth and blocked it, the piece should not grow any more, as it has been maxed out.

● **TIP** HANGING IT UP

Sometimes, if there is a combination of factors such as inelastic yarn and a loosened gauge or super bulky and inelastic yarn, I'll even weigh down the swatch slightly with some wooden clothespins or some jewelry such as earrings or brooches to mimic the pull on a greater length of knitted fabric. Let's say the garment is 24 inches (61cm) long total. If you've made your swatch 6 inches (15cm) square, figure that you will need the equivalent of three more swatches hanging from the bottom. This total of four 6-inch (15cm) swatches represents the final length.

6" x 6" swatch = 1/4 oz

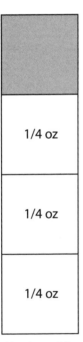

1/4 oz

1/4 oz

1/4 oz

Hanging swatches

Weighing In

Now go weigh your swatch. I've been known to go to the post office or the supermarket, where there are very accurate scales, but you may have a food scale at home. Let's say your 6-inch (15cm) swatch weighs 1/4 ounce (7g). Now multiply three swatches by 1/4 ounce (7g) for a total weight of 3/4 ounce (21g) pulling down on your top swatch. Use the scale to find out how many clothespins or earrings or brooches make up 3/4 ounce (21g). Hang your swatch overnight with this amount of weight evenly distributed across the bottom. Take off the weights and let it rest while hanging for a few hours. Now take the swatch measurement.

The reason for hanging with stuff on, then off, is to take the average. The second swatch from the top only has two swatches, or 1/2 ounce (14g), pulling it down. The second from the bottom only has one swatch hanging from it, or 1/4 ounce (7g). The very bottom swatch has absolutely nothing hanging on the bottom of it. Does it make sense to have all and none for the average?

The real process, then, is to wash, block, hang. Again, I say wash, block, hang. I know this is not very spontaneous. I know only too well how we all chomp at the bit to begin a new project. However, there is a critical line

found in many directions, which usually appears under the gauge information: "To save time, take time to make the swatch." I'd amend it and say, "To save time, take time to make the swatch and to wash, block, and hang it."

Using Your Swatch to Estimate Your Yarn Needs

You may think you make a swatch just to determine your tension or gauge, but the swatch can give you lots of other useful information, too. You know now that it will tell you about the washability, wearability, and colorfastness of the yarn, and whether the knitted fabric will shrink or grow; but it can also help you estimate your yarn needs.

Say you find a cute stitch in a stitch dictionary and want to create a simple piece without shaping, such as a scarf or a stole or a blanket, without a pattern. How do you know the amount of yarn required? If you figure out about how big the finished piece will be, you can use the weight of your 6-inch (15cm) swatch to estimate the weight of the yarn you will need. Fold up a tablecloth or a sheet or a piece of fabric to the width and length you want your scarf or shawl to be.

Suppose you decide your scarf will be 12 inches (30.5cm) wide by 72 inches (183cm)

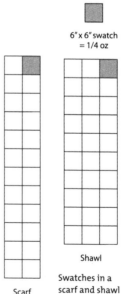

6" x 6" swatch = 1/4 oz

Scarf

Shawl

Swatches in a scarf and shawl

long. How many 6-inch (15cm) square swatches will fit in your project? There will be an equivalent of two across by twelve down for a total of twenty-four swatches. If each swatch is $1/4$ ounce (7g), then twenty-four times $1/4$ ounce (7g) means 6 ounces (170g) of yarn is required for your scarf.

A stole that is 18 inches (45.5cm) wide by 60 inches (152.5cm) long will require the equivalent of thirty swatches (three swatches across by ten down) at $1/4$ ounce (7g) per swatch, or $7^1/2$ ounces (213g) of yarn. Can you figure out the yarn needed for an afghan measuring 48 inches (122cm) by 60 inches (152.5cm)? A food scale that can weigh the swatch in grams will give an even more accurate measurement of the weight. Instead of looking at swatching as a chore, it now looks like a pretty useful thing, doesn't it?

YARN REQUIREMENTS FOR A SWEATER

When designing something more complex, such as a sweater, take all of the measurements you have in mind for the garment and apply the same principle. Let's say the sweater is 42 inches (106.5cm) wide overall—21 inches (53.5cm) each for the front and back—and 24 inches (61cm) long. The sleeves will be 18 inches (45.5cm) long, 9 inches (23cm) wide at the cuffs, and 18

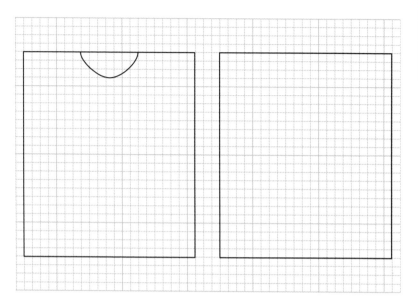

A sweater's measurements on graph paper

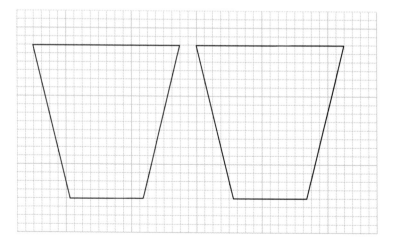

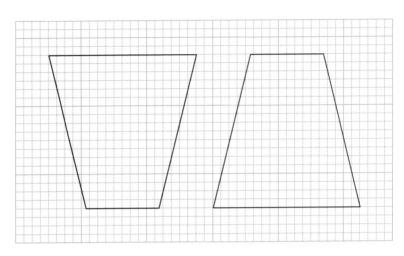

Two sleeves:
one turned up-
side down

inches (45.5cm) wide at the top. Put all these measurements on a piece of square-grid graph paper (not knitting graph paper) where each box represents one inch (2.5cm).

Now figure out how many 6-inch (15cm) square swatches fit into the sweater. Here's a quick way to do that: Just cut out several squares of the same graph paper that are six boxes by six boxes, lay them over the drawing of the sweater, and count! Keep careful count of how many boxes you use, and use the bits and pieces from the ones you cut to fit for the sleeves. This is a boon to the mathematically impaired.

Here's the math. There are seven swatches that fit across both front and back pieces and four vertically for a total of twenty-eight

6-inch (15cm) swatches in the full body. For the sleeves, turn one sleeve upside down and place it next to the right-side-up sleeve to make a parallelogram. (A parallelogram has the same formula for area as a rectangle, or height times width.)

This parallelogram is 27 inches (69cm) across (cuff plus top), or four-and-a-half swatches wide, and 18 inches (45.5cm) long, or three swatches vertically. So, three times four and a half equals thirteen-and-a-half swatches needed for both sleeves. Add this to the twenty-eight from the body, and the entire sweater requires forty-one-and-a-half 6-inch (15cm) square swatches. Multiply this by the $1/4$ ounce (7g) per swatch and you get $10^3/8$ ounces (294g) of yarn needed for the sweater.

Even though you will need a little less yarn since you won't be knitting the neck opening, you may need extra yarn for the neckband; and it's always good to have yarn just in case, so this estimate is pretty accurate.

Using Your Swatches

You will always find a use for the swatch.

- I know knitters are very generous and knit a lot of things to give away, so start a knitting scrapbook. Keep a record of the yarn and needle size; take a picture of the finished item and keep it with the swatch. After all, that swatch may be the only sou venir you have left of the project.

- Conversely, give the swatch to the recipient as a taste of things to come. How often have you missed a deadline? That baby sweater not finished? Well, maybe the kid is now in college. The wedding afghan a bit late? They're getting a divorce already. Perhaps I exaggerate; but if I cannot get the gift out in a timely fashion, I'll give the swatch to show the recipient what's in store.

- Make something new. Collect your swatches to piece together for a patch work afghan or throw. Or fold the swatch in half, sew the sides together, and attach a small zipper to the top to make a coin purse.

- You can wash the swatch every time you launder the project so you will always have matching yarn should you need to mend the knitted item later.

- Or you can do what most knitters do with their swatches—rip out the yarn and use it in the project, which is great, especially if you run short. Most yarn can handle being gently ripped out and reused. However, repeatedly ripping and reknitting it can make it look worn. If you need to make several swatches, use a new ball each time to limit the wear on any one length of yarn.

If you rip out your swatch to use the yarn again, you may need to straighten it out because the loops formed by knitting have crimped the yarn. To remove these kinks, wind the yarn loosely in a hank, perhaps around a stretched-out wire coat hanger, tie it in several places (page 88), then dunk it in water until it's thoroughly wet. Squeeze out the water and hang the hank in the bathroom until dry, then rewind. Do *not* weigh it down to remove kinks; that can stretch it out and result in yarn that won't stretch as much as the rest of the balls, giving an uneven result after the next blocking.

Making a swatch also helps you see how the yarn works up in a particular stitch and how you feel about it. That stitch pattern may be very pretty to look at, but you may find that working it is a pain. Swatching allows you to sample the stitch pattern to see if you can live with it for the next several weeks. I call these the "trophy wife" stitches—pretty to look at but very high maintenance!

Adjusting Garment Lengths

The most flattering length of a sweater for almost every body is one that hits at around the hipbone. Often, the lengths given in a pattern or set of instructions are not right for us. For me, the right length is 20 inches (51cm). To measure yourself, put a tape measure at the highest point on the shoulder (right next to the neck), and let it fall to the hipbone—that's your preferred length. An alternative is to take any garment whose length you like and measure it.

Now you can make the adjustments to the pattern according to your length. Almost all patterns today come with an illustrated set of measurements called a schematic. Choose the size you want to make and draw those measurements on square graph paper, with each box equal to one inch (2.5cm). Do this in pencil so that you can erase any errors later.

All adjustments to length—one of the easiest changes to make to a pattern—should occur below the armholes. That way, the armholes stay the same size and the sleeves will still fit into them. Make the changes to the schematic for your length so you know how long to make the body before you have to begin the armhole shaping.

Pattern schematics on graph paper

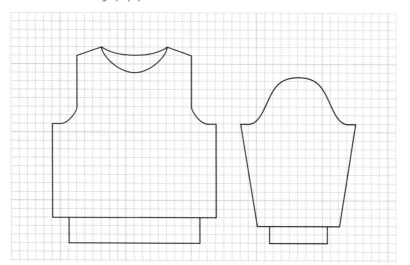

New schematics adjusted for length

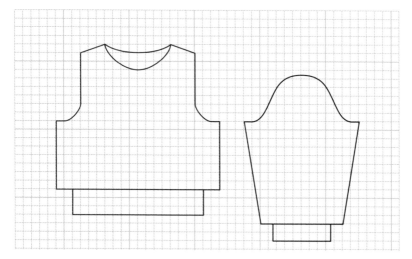

Standard ribbing proportions

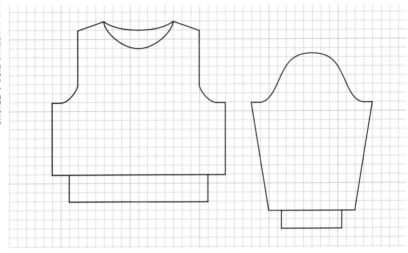

But wait, there's more. Most patterns call for a standard 3 inches (7.5cm) of ribbing on the body and 2 inches (5cm) of ribbing for the sleeves. But you can change this. Experiment with proportions that please your eye: Try a modern high-waisted ribbing for an empire line or minimal ribs for a funkier look. Just keep in mind that the ribbing also works to keep the edges from curling, and there may be a minimum needed to avoid that flip-up. You can knit a swatch to see how it works. Remember that adjustments to sleeve length mean refiguring how often to increase (for example, every fourth row so many times, then every sixth row so many times, and so on).

Changes to ribbing proportions

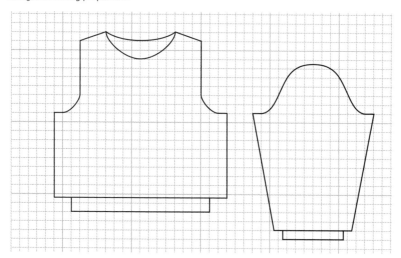

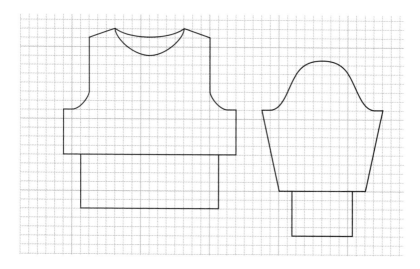

● **TIP** FINDING THE #%^!$#@%~ CENTER
OF THE BALL OF YARN

We all prefer to have what is known as a center-pull skein so that the ball of yarn does not roll around as we work; but sometimes the strand coming out of the center of a ball or skein is not evident, and we have to go in and fish for it, usually ending up pulling out a huge wad of yarn that's almost half the skein.

To find the center more easily, go in from either end of the ball. Insert your fingers into the top and bottom of the skein, almost like Chinese handcuffs. When your fingers meet, you know you're in the center. Now twirl a finger around and feel for the inner spiral, grab the yarn closest to the inside, and pull it out. You should be able to pull out a pinch of yarn, without a lot of excess.

Finding the center of
a ball of yarn

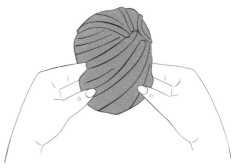

Working with Coned Yarns

. . . .

Coned yarns are a lot more economical to use than skeins. I also love the fact that with a cone you don't need to join separate skeins, so there are fewer ends to weave in. Coned yarn is often used for machine knitting and/or weaving; and to facilitate their movement through the machine, the yarn is sometimes treated with some kind of wax or oil that smoothes the stray fibers and flattens the plies together. The yarn is under tension as it is wound onto a cone, so by the time it gets to the knitter, coned knitting yarn is often tamped down by the wax and stretched out from being wound on the cone.

If you knit with coned yarns as is, you will see a remarkable transformation when you wash your swatch (and you *do* swatch, don't you?). The wax washes away, the yarn springs back, and the swatch fluffs up to fill empty spaces. Some yarns that appear limp and lifeless are transformed into something wonderfully soft and springy. You can really see how much the yarn has "decompressed."

TO WASH OR NOT TO WASH. If you prewash the yarn, you will have softer and springier yarn to work with rather than the stringier and less-than-satisfying off-the-cone feeling. Before you wash the yarn, wind it into hanks

Hank of yarn

around the back of a chair and tie it in at least four places, evenly spaced, with smooth, contrasting cotton. Now hand-wash the yarn as you would the finished product (not in the washing machine) and let it dry flat and unstretched. Rewind the yarn into a ball either by hand or by using a yarn winder. I know, you're saying that there are too many extra steps and you want to begin the project already. Have I told you how awfully soft prewashed cashmere can be compared to the limp and unwashed version?

● **TIP** SETTING UP CONED YARN

If you are going to use coned yarn straight from the cone, which works well with cotton, reeling the yarn off the cone is often problematic since pulling on it sideways usually results in the cone toppling over.

You can use a floor lamp and have the yarn feed upward first, then horizontally over the lamp. Or try a small lazy Susan so that the yarn feeds off horizontally when the lazy Susan spins around.

GOING CONELESS. I often push the cardboard cone out to make the yarn almost like a large center-pull ball. To do this, I sit in a chair and place the upside-down cone on the floor between my feet. I push downward with my feet as I pull the cardboard cone up and out of the yarn. If it doesn't come out easily, sometimes I try to pull it out with pliers or I may hammer down on the cone from the top. If it still refuses to come out, I just use the floor lamp method.

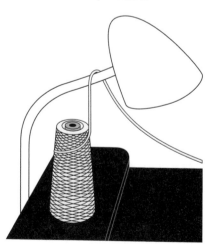

Coned yarn
set-up

A Better Cast-On— Using Mathematics

When making a long-tail cast-on, a perennial favorite of knitters, the big question is how much yarn to reel off. Too much and there is waste, which you do not want to do, especially with the price of yarn. Too little and you won't be able to make enough stitches. Some say to use two different balls for casting on, but that means two extra ends to weave in later.

The general rule is to reel off three times the width of your piece, and add 10 percent of the original width. For instance, for an 8-inch (20.5cm)-wide scarf, you will need at least 24 inches (61cm) of yarn for the tail plus another .8 for a total of 24.8 inches (63cm)—or about 25 inches (63.5cm). For a 22-inch (56cm)-wide sweater front, you will reel off 66 inches (168cm) plus another 2.2 for a total of 68.2 inches (173cm)—or about 69 inches (175cm).

One could arrive at this conclusion through trial and error, but the reason it works is actually grounded in mathematics. Looking at a stitch, the loop on the needle is almost a circle. There is a formula in math that says if you know the widest part of a circle (the diameter), then you can figure out the length

around the outside of the circle (the circumference) by multiplying the width by a magic
number called pi, or 3.14159. So, reel off an
amount following this formula and you
should not run out of yarn tail.

Circumference

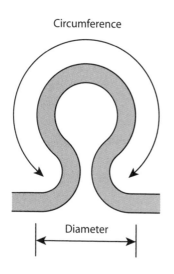

The loop of
a stitch

Diameter

● **TIP** GAINING EXTRA STITCHES

Suppose you reel off the amount suggested above and still run out of yarn in the tail, and you curse me while muttering under your breath. What went wrong? If you work the long-tail method very slowly, you'll see which yarn actually ends up wrapping around the needle. For the slingshot method, it is the yarn held on the index finger. For the two-handed method, it is the right-hand yarn. The other yarn (the thumb loop and the left-hand yarn respectively) actually makes an underlining loop for the one on the needle. In essence, the long-tail cast-on is really casting on and knitting the first row at the same time. Hence the use of the two strands. The thumb loop, or the left-hand yarn, is actually doing what is known as the half-hitch, or backward loop, cast-on (page 41).

It stands to reason that you will use a bit more of the yarn from the strand that winds up on the needle and less from the strand that forms the underlining loop, or half hitch. So, think of the two Ts: Be sure to keep the Tail on your Thumb when making this cast-on. Since this part of the cast-on uses a bit less yarn, you should then never run out.

● **TIP** KNITTING CONTINENTALLY

I run into many knitters who knit by throwing the yarn with their right hand. I actually am more comfortable knitting this way myself. They express a desire to learn how to knit Continental-style, by holding the yarn with the left hand. Guess what? If you know how to do the long-tail cast-on in the slingshot method, you are really knitting "continentally." Remember when I said to pretend the left thumb is like your left needle?

You then insert the right-hand needle into the left-thumb loop as if to knit and scoop the yarn from the left index finger. Isn't this what Continental knitters do? They hold their yarn over the left index finger and scoop the yarn in the same manner. You are really knitting this first row Continental-style. It's Continental purl that can be a pain.

Yarn for Seaming

If you are casting on for a piece such as a sweater that will require a seam, you can add seaming yarn to your tail and eliminate an extra two ends to weave in later (one from the cast-on and one from the joined seaming yarn). You should reel off one-and-a-half times the length of the seam for mattress seaming. For example, if a sweater back will have a side seam of 12 inches

(30.5cm), reel off an extra 18 inches (45.5cm) for seaming yarn. For backstitch seaming, which I personally seldom do, triple the length of the seam and reel off 36 inches (91cm).

● TIP BREAD-TIE BOBBIN

Of course, you know what happens, right? After casting on, you wind up knitting with the tail of the seaming yarn. Many knitters roll up the long tail into a ball, which either becomes all knotted up or gets loose and starts to fall apart. To prevent accidentally knitting with the tail/seaming yarn and to keep the seaming yarn clean and tidy without knotting while you work, use a notched plastic bread tie that comes with most plastic-bagged bakery products. I've saved these ties for years. Look at these as free mini bobbins, perfect to wrap seaming yarn onto. Just don't take them off the bread on the supermarket shelves—that's not nice.

Bread-tie
bobbins

● **TIP** RUNNING SHORT AND PURLING ON

Say you need to cast on 288 stitches. For whatever reason—perhaps the stars are misaligned or the moon is waning—you get to stitch 282 and run out of tail yarn. You thought you reeled off a little more than three times the width, and you're sure you kept the "tail on the thumb" (page 92). What are you going to do? Well, cry and curse of course; but will you rip out the 282 stitches you've already cast on? Of course not.

Turn the piece around as if to work the next row. Notice that there are purl bumps on this side. Why are they there? Well, remember that you knitted the other side as you created the cast-on. (A lot of knitters are bothered by the look of this, so after casting on in long-tail, they make the first

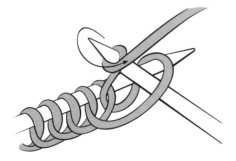

Purling on stitches

Purled on
stitches added
to cast-on

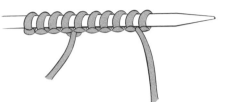

row the wrong side.) However, if it looks like a purl and it smells like a purl and it probably tastes like a purl, I say purl your stitches on. That is, purl into the first stitch without taking that stitch off the left-hand needle. Instead, place your new stitch that's on the right-hand needle onto the left-hand needle in order to gain a new stitch. Tighten it slightly for tension. *Now purl into this new first stitch and place the next new stitch you create onto the left-hand needle as well. Repeat from * until you get the number of stitches you need.

The result is not totally like the other cast-on stitches. It lacks the full underlining loop, so it is slightly thinner. It's very close, however, and I guarantee you it's a much better solution than ripping out 282 stitches and starting over. Besides, these extra few stitches wind up at the corner of the afghan or at the lower side seam of a garment. Who'll know?

Casting On in Pattern

You know that you can knit your stitches on
(page 46), and now you've seen that you can
purl them on, too. Using both methods, you
can cast on in pattern. That way, unlike with
the long-tail cast-on, the pattern will go all
the way down to the lower edges.

There are ways to knit and purl using the
long-tail cast-on, too, but this method is
very accessible. This cast-on is not as
stretchy as the long-tail, however, and the
only yarn to reel off here is any seaming
yarn that may be needed later.

To cast on in pattern, place a slip knot on
the left-hand needle. *Purl* into this slip knot
and place the new stitch from the right-hand
needle back onto the left-hand needle.
There are now two stitches total, the original
slip knot and this newly purled-on stitch.
* *Knit* into the first stitch on the left-hand
needle (actually the one just made); place
the new stitch from the right-hand needle
back onto the left-hand needle for one more
stitch. *Purl* into the new first stitch on the
left-hand needle and place the stitch from
the right-hand needle back onto the left-hand
needle for one more stitch. Rep from * until
you cast on the number of stitches you need.

Casting on
in pattern

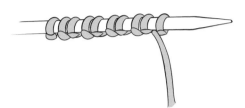

This method can be used for 1 x 1 ribbing (knit 1, purl 1); the undulation of the rib is already evident. Use it for seed stitch or moss stitch as well, and then knit the purls and purl the knits. Work 2 x 2 ribbing by knitting on two stitches, then purling on two. You can work any combination of knits and purls: Try a 5 x 3 rib or a 4 x 4 basket weave (which alternates rows of knit 4 and purl 4).

Crocheted Cast-On

I adapted this method of casting on, which I sometimes call chaining on, in 1988 from machine knitting (yet again), and in recent years it's become more popular with hand knitters. It is not very stretchy, so it's good for stable edges on scarves, afghans, or handbags. The great advantage is that it will match any knitted bind-off. And this cast-on can also be used for what is known as the temporary, or provisional, cast-on; but more on this later.

You will use a crochet hook the same size as your needle (Know Your Hook, page 101) to make a crocheted chain around the needle. Again, as with knitting/purling on in pattern, the only yarn to reel off is any seaming yarn if it will be needed later. Make a slip knot and place it on the crochet hook. With the hook in the right hand and the knitting needle in the left, *bring the yarn behind the needle from below and to the front from above the needle. Catch the yarn with the hook and pull it through to form a chain—one stitch is cast on. Repeat from * until you have one fewer stitch than called for, then move the loop on the crochet hook onto the needle. So if the directions call for casting on ninety-nine stitches, chain on only ninety-eight, then add the loop from the hook as the last stitch.

This cast-on creates a full chain at the bottom and is a perfect match to any bind-off, which, after all, looks like a chain. This is especially important on items such as a scarf, where both ends are in view and you want the top to match the bottom. Most of all, it forms a smoother bottom, and who wouldn't like a smoother bottom?

A bonus to this method is that you can pick up stitches from the cast-on edge later more easily. If you are going to add trim, just

Crocheted cast-on

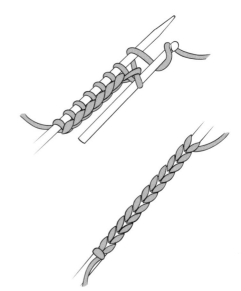

insert the needle into the bottom-edge chain, which is sturdy and easy to distinguish. Use this cast-on method for those instances where you begin in the middle of the project and must later pick up and work downward from the cast-on edge for symmetry on the other side.

● **TIP** KNOW YOUR HOOK

How do you know that a crochet hook is the same size as your knitting needle if it is not labeled with both a letter and a number? You could try rolling the hook and needle around together in the palms of your hands to see if they feel about the same thickness.

In a pinch (for American sizes only), remember that H is 8. They almost rhyme. If you know that H is 8, you can go up and down from there. That means size I is a 9, J is a 10, and K is a $10\frac{1}{2}$. G is a 7, F is a 6, and so on. You can start from the beginning with A is a 1, B is a 2; but most yarn and needle sizes we gravitate toward are right in the middle, or at H/8.

Trying to stick the hook through a gauge check (page 18) is not always the best idea because with some hooks the heads are bigger than the shafts, which is where the size is measured.

Chained Provisional Cast-On

Another use for the chained cast-on is to work a provisional, or temporary, cast-on, which you will rip out later in order to work from the live stitches, or the stitches still to be worked at the bottom of the piece. A provisional cast-on is usually worked in a contrasting waste yarn. I like to use a smooth cotton that is the same weight, or thickness, as the working yarn but in a contrasting color, which will make it easier to remove later.

For a provisional cast-on, make a slip knot with the waste yarn and chain on exactly the number of stitches you need over the knitting needle as in the crocheted cast-on (page 99). If the instructions say to cast on ninety-nine stitches, chain on ninety-nine stitches. Then make a few extra chains with just the yarn and the crochet hook without going around the needle.

Break the waste yarn and elongate the last loop on the crochet hook. You don't want to fasten and end off because you will be taking the chain out from this end later.

Switch to the project yarn. Work and complete the item.

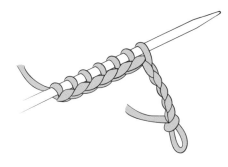

Chained provisional cast-on

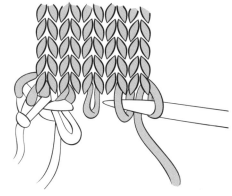

Pulling out the provisional cast-on

YANKING YOUR CHAIN (as it were). Remember that last elongated loop made after cutting the waste yarn? Now that the knitting is complete, that's what you'll be pulling. Have an extra knitting needle handy. Pull out the chain until the underside of the first cast-on stitch is freed up and place this loop onto the extra needle. Continue to unravel each chain and place the freed-up loop from each un-raveled chain onto the needle.

Most standard directions for doing a provisional, or temporary, cast-on tell you to loosely make a chain with the scrap yarn, then to pick up a stitch from the back side, or the purl bump, of the chain.

This purl bump is often hard to pick out, and the chain can become tight and difficult to work into. Not only that, but the chain can twist around and make pulling it out later difficult. By using the chain-on method with the waste yarn, there's no need to fish for this little back bump because this back loop of the chain is already over the needle, so the back bumps are there waiting for you with no need to hunt for them later.

A traditional provisional cast-on

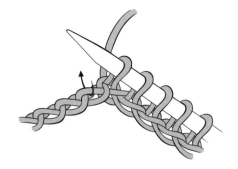

Crochet Chain Cast-On Variation

While the previous crochet cast-on forms a full chain across the bottom, this method does not. But this cast-on is stretchier, and the bottom is not as bulky. Here the loop does not stay on the hook but gets placed on the needle.

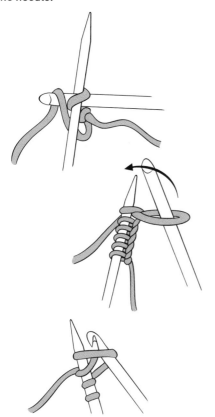

Another way of chaining on stitches

To begin, make a slip knot and place it on the knitting needle, which is in your left hand. Insert the crochet hook, which is in your right hand, into the slip knot as if to knit, wrap the yarn around the hook and draw through the slip-knot loop as if to make a chain but do *not* remove the slip knot from needle. Instead, place the loop from the crochet hook onto the needle to create a second stitch. *Insert the crochet hook into the new stitch as if to knit, wrap the yarn around the hook, and draw

Chained-on
stitches

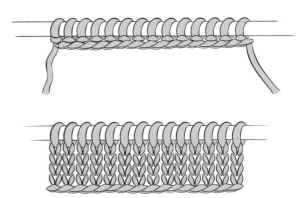

through the stitch as if to make a chain but do not remove the stitch from the needle. Instead, place the loop from the crochet hook onto the needle to create another stitch. Repeat from * until you have the desired number of stitches.

The result looks like you've gone into the top loop only of a crocheted chain and picked up a stitch from there, and it's identical to the knitted cast-on (page 46). It's easy to pick up stitches from the bottom cast-on edge later, though this will not be entirely undetectable afterward.

● **TIP** JOINING IN THE ROUND
       WITHOUT TWISTING

You use a circular needle primarily to work in the round without having to seam, but the term circular knitting is a bit of a misnomer. As the last stitch meets up with the first stitch, in order for you to continue on, you must make a "jump" by working over to the first stitch, so it should be called spiral knitting instead. After casting on, directions will tell you to join, being careful not to twist. With all those stitches squeezed onto the skinny nylon cable portion of the knitting needle, this is easier said than done.

I use old-fashioned wooden clothespins and work on a large pillow placed on my lap. Every so many stitches, let's say twenty or thirty, I place a clothespin on the stitches to hold the bottom edge to the inside of the needle. When finished, I make sure that the clothespins are all facing the same way.

The truth is, you don't have to check to see that your stitches are not twisted until you have completed one row. The single, lonely strand holding together the beginning and the end can still twirl around. Even though you checked that your knitting wasn't twisted when you first joined the round, it can (and will) twist again while knitting the second round. Check again before you start the third round and then straighten out the round if need be. You should be fine after that.

If the clothespin method does not appeal to you, don't join the knitting immediately after casting on. Work two rows back and forth—not circularly—to get more sub-stance to the bottom before you join the ends. Use the end tail to seam these few rows. Note, however, that the stitches may look somewhat different when worked back and forth than when worked circularly.

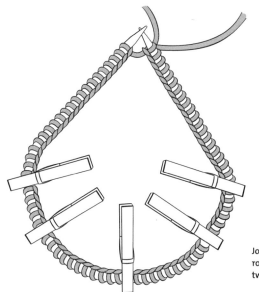

Joining in the round without twisting

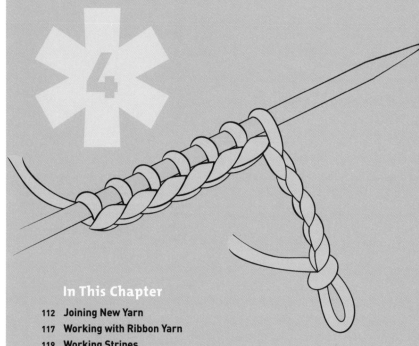

In This Chapter

112 **Joining New Yarn**

117 **Working with Ribbon Yarn**

119 **Working Stripes**

121 **Intarsia Color Changes**

122 **Knitting in Pictures**

125 **Decreases**

125 Knit 2 Together (k2tog)

126 Slip, Slip, Knit (ssk)

127 Slip, Knit, Pass Stitch Over (skp)

127 Knit 2 Together Through the
      Back Loop (k2tog tbl)

128 Left-Slanting Decrease

132 **Increases**

132 Knit in Front and Back (kf&b)

137 **Fixing Mistakes**

137 Duplicate Stitch

142 Dropping Stitches to Fix a Cable

As You Work

You are bound to **run into snags,** be puzzled by some instructions, or just need to get past a sticky place as you are knitting; and these **hints** and tips will provide the tools for you to do just that. So now you can sit back and **enjoy** your knitting!

Joining New Yarn

At some point, you will run out of yarn and have to introduce a new ball or skein. Or perhaps you want to make stripes, where you have to attach a new color. In either case, the goal is to try to make this change at the edges of the piece or the beginning or end of a row. Traditionally, we are told to begin the new yarn (either a new color or more of the same yarn) by just starting with the new stuff, leaving enough tail to weave in later. I don't know about you, but I always get rather nervous about this. I have visions of the whole piece unraveling. And the last stitch of the old ball and the first stitch of the new ball are always loose and sloppy. And how annoying is it to accidentally start to work with the long end rather than with the new ball of yarn?

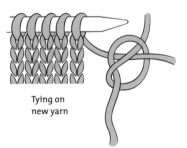

Tying on
new yarn

TIE ONE ON. Don't just let those ends dangle. Instead, let me suggest that you tie one on. No, vodka is not involved. Just wrap the new yarn around the old one and tie a simple knot. The knot of new yarn should slide up and down the old yarn. Just snuggle the yarn up close to the stitch and continue working with the new yarn.

"Knot" only will this prevent raveling while working, but the stitches are in there nicely and firmly. If the thought of any knots at all bothers you, not to worry. It's the simplest knot you can make; and after completing the project, you can easily take it out and weave in the ends. However, since it's not a bulky knot and it's at the edge, you can also keep it in there if you like and hide it in the trim or in a seam. Another advantage to knotting the yarn is that the tail does not need to be excessively long, so you will never mistake it for yarn from the ball and begin working with the wrong end. The one time you would leave a longer tail is when working wide stripes in a piece that will be seamed later. Then it's advantageous to leave a long enough tail to sew up that stripe to its corresponding stripe from the other side with the same color seaming yarn.

There are those who champion working the first few stitches with both strands held together, but this makes those stitches too bulky. And it will not work well if you're changing colors because these few stitches at the beginning will be made up of both colors.

● **TIP** MEASURING YARN FOR ONE ROW

How do you know how much yarn will get you to the end of the row? As you approach the end of the yarn ball, start keeping track of exactly how many yards you need to

make one row. Reel off 5–10 yards (4.5–9m) at a time and place a slip knot on the yarn to mark the reeled-off yardage. On a piece of paper, keep track of how many yards have been reeled off with old-fashioned ticks or hash marks.

This will also help you towards the end of your project. If you're running out of yarn altogether, you can now project how many more rows are necessary before you complete the project and how much yarn that entails. If you see that there is not enough yarn left, you can either go to the store immediately to buy more or find some other solution, such as adding trim in another color or another yarn.

● TIP SPIT SPLICING

If you are using yarns made of animal fiber that can be felted (not superwash yarns), you can use a technique known as the spit splice. As the name implies, you felt the two ends of yarns together by spitting on them and rapidly rolling them together between the palms of your hands. If this does not sound palatable, use warm water—soapy water is even better. I like to fray the ends for 2–3 inches (5–7.5cm) first to ensure good contact. I then remove about half the amount of fiber from each frayed end so that

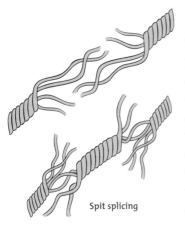

Spit splicing

when combined, the two ends are the same thickness as the yarn. I try to intertwine the remaining ends together, wet them, and then roll them.

This technique is best used for same-colored yarns because finding the exact point where one should change colors is too tricky, plus blending two colors would present the same visual problems as knitting with both tails. Make the spit splice several yards before you need it to allow the ends to dry. Never spit splice after drinking coffee or red wine, for obvious reasons.

● TIP NEEDLE FELTING

If you are using nonfelting, nonanimal fibers, needle felting is a way of joining the ends together with a surprisingly strong hold. I've used this method on man-made fibers and cotton. To do this, you will need a felting needle—a long, very sharp needle with barbs at one end—and something protective such as a thick piece of foam to place under the yarn to be felted. You fray, halve, and intertwine the yarn ends as you did for spit splicing, then punch up and down with the needle repeatedly, which drives the fibers through each other, causing them to adhere together. The results are a bit fuzzy, but I cut off the fuzzy bits and continue.

The Russian join

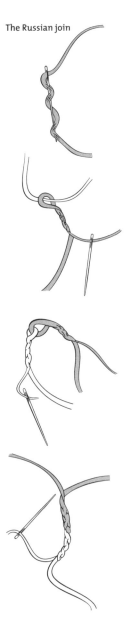

● **TIP** THE RUSSIAN JOIN

Another alternative for joining yarns made of nonanimal fibers is the Russian join. Here the two yarn ends loop around each other, then each takes a U-turn and is woven into itself with a tapestry or smaller darning needle. Halve or thin out both ends, as described in spit splicing, for about 4 inches (10cm). Since each strand gets "buried" back onto itself, it can work for color changes if you carefully figure out the exact place of the join.

Begin with one yarn, threading the halved end onto a tapestry needle and weaving it back into the yarn itself, forming a small loop. Leave a little bit of the tail of the halved end accessible. Thread the other yarn end through the loop of the first yarn and with a darning needle weave this yarn onto itself leaving a small loop. Now pull on the halved tail ends of each yarn to close up both small loops and trim off the remaining tail ends.

Working with Ribbon Yarn

Ribbon yarns are so pretty in the skein, yet they seem to totally lose their flat, smooth texture when they are knitted. Part of this is due to the twisting of the ribbon as it comes off the ball, which can be so irritating.

Think about it. Does toilet paper ever twist? No. So why not apply the same principle to dispense ribbon or tape yarn and help alleviate some of this twisting. To make a ribbon dispenser, take an old shoe box and a straight knitting needle, any size. Pierce the outside of the shoe box with the needle, place the ball of ribbon onto the needle, then pierce the other side of the shoe box so that the ribbon hangs inside the shoe box.

You'll still get some twisting as you knit because the ribbon will twist or fold as it

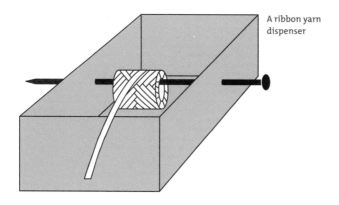

A ribbon yarn dispenser

encircles the needle for each stitch, but it will be a lot less twisted than when the ribbon is just pulled from a free-standing ball.

● **TIP** JOINING RIBBON YARNS

When joining the ends of ribbon yarn, even the smallest of knots will be too bulky. I overlap the ends of ribbon about $^1/_8$ inch (3mm) and sew them together with a sewing needle and matching thread for an imperceptible, bulk-free joining. There are several advantages: no ends to weave in (important since lots of ribbon yarns are slippery), no waste (great since ribbon tends to be pricy), and the sewing stitches will prevent fraying at the ribbon ends.

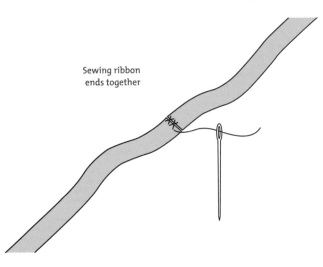

Sewing ribbon
ends together

Working Stripes

One of the easiest ways to dress up a project is to change colors every few rows to create horizontal stripes. (To add a new color yarn, see page 112.) If the stripes are narrow—that is, if you change colors every two rows or four rows—don't cut the color not being used but carry it up along the side edge. This forms a short "float" of the non-working yarn. Do not pull up these floats too tightly or this edge will bunch up and become distorted. Do not leave the floats too loose or the edge will be sloppy and things can get caught.

Notice how stripes are usually worked in even-numbered row combinations. That's because you must get back to the same edge where the other yarn is waiting to be used next. This is not the case when working circularly in rounds, where stripes can be added in odd-numbered increments, too.

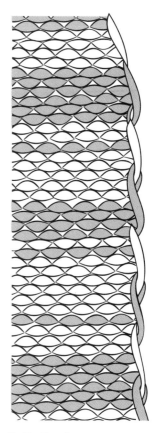

Floating threads along a side edge of striped knitting

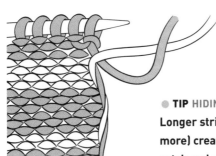

Hiding the
floats

● **TIP** HIDING LONG FLOATS

Longer stripes of six or eight rows (or more) create floats that are too long and will catch and snag. Ending off the yarn and rejoining means more ends to weave in, and who wants that? The solution is to catch the yarn not being used at the edge of the work.

To do that, just lay the nonworking yarn *over* the working yarn before beginning the new row. You can lay the nonworking yarn from front to back or from back to front, just keep it consistent. Now you can work stripes of six or eight rows—even twelve or twenty-four rows—without ever having to end off and reattach yarns, and you'll have very few ends to weave in. Check on the tension of the floats as you work so the edge does not become distorted.

Intarsia Color Changes

Intarsia, which is known also as picture knitting, and "color blocks" both involve working sections of different colors that require changing colors in the middle of a row. When joining the new color yarn, tie it on (page 112). However, leaving a knot in the middle of your work is never a good idea so you can take the knot out later and weave in the end.

The much maligned intarsia technique involves winding the different colors onto bobbins or plastic yarn holders (page 94) ahead of time. At the place where the two colors meet, the yarns must wrap around each other to prevent a hole from developing. To do this, twist the yarns around each other before starting with the new color.

Color change in the middle of a row

Front

Back

Knitting in Pictures

. . . .

You can take the instructions for a plain stockinette stitch project and create your own picture charts. Intarsia does little to change the gauge of stockinette, so go ahead and "color in" your sweaters or afghans. One of the easiest ways to create charts is to use knitter's gauge graph paper. The proportions of these boxes are not square; instead they are rectangles, short and wide, just like knit stitches.

Think about this. What are some typical gauges? Four stitches and six rows to the inch? Five stitches and seven rows per inch? Six stitches and eight rows to the inch? Notice that the stitch count is always the smaller number and the row count is the larger number. Think of knit stitches as little Porky Pigs: They are short and wide. Just how wide are they? They are so fat that it takes four of them side by side to create an inch. Yet they are so short that you need six of them standing on each other's shoulders to achieve the same inch. If you charted your greyhound dog on square graph paper and knitted it, you'd get a dachshund.

You can find such proportioned graph paper on the Internet by searching for "knit gauge graph paper." You can also use a program called Print-A-Grid from Knitting Software. Use a graphic or illustration in a size that's knittable, in other words, not postage stamp size. Photocopy the grid onto some clear sheets of acetate at a copy shop or on your own printer.

Now lay the clear sheet over the graphic and color in the boxes with crayons or markers that will draw on the acetate. Color in any box that's at least half of that particular color. You've now converted the graphic to a chart from which to work.

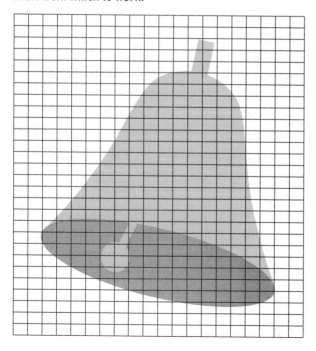

Placing knitter's graph paper over a design

As an alternative you could print your graphics onto a sheet of knitter's graph paper. There will be boxes that are partially filled with color, and you'll have to determine what color it should be and fully color in that stitch.

If you are really particular, photocopy your swatch of knitting and color in the actual stitches to preview what your picture will look like knitted up. Make sure your swatch is light enough in color or the stitches will be too dark to color over.

Photocopy of actual knitting stitches colored in

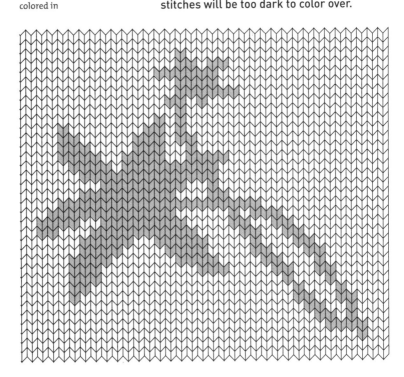

Decreases

· ·

When you shape a piece such as an armhole or a neckline, you decrease (dec) by reducing the number of stitches. The quickest and easiest way to do this is to knit two stitches together (k2tog), but there are other stitch techniques to use.

Knit 2 Together (k2tog)

Insert your needle into the next two stitches and work them as one. You will have one less stitch.

This puts the second of these two stitches on top of the first, and this decrease leans upward to the right; it is a right-slanting decrease. For symmetry, we aim for what are known as matched, or paired, decreases; that is, on the other side of the neck or for that other armhole, we would then work a left-slanting decrease. This means having the first stitch wind up over the second.

Knit 2 together

Slip, Slip, Knit (ssk)

Slip, slip, knit—or ssk—is the most pre-scribed way to work a left-slanting decrease. Slip the first stitch off the left-hand needle onto the right-hand needle as if to knit, slip the second stitch off in the same way, then insert the left-hand needle into the fronts of both slipped stitches and knit them together in this position, also known as knitting through their *back* loops (tbl), or legs. Slipping knitwise (kwise) changes the orien-tation of the stitches (page 47) first so they won't be twisted after knitting through the back loops.

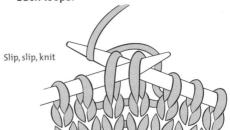

Slip, slip, knit

Slip, knit, pass
stitch over

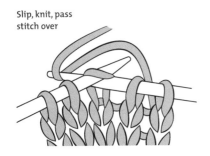

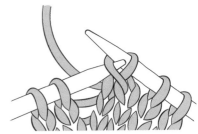

Slip, Knit, Pass Stitch Over (skp)

A more old-fashioned way of performing a left-slanting decrease is called slip, knit, pass stitch over, or skp (sometimes sl1k1psso). Slip the first stitch off the left-hand needle and onto the right-hand needle knitwise, knit the next stitch, then use the tip of the left-hand needle to lift the first stitch (the slipped one) and pass it over the second (the knitted one). Lifting the slipped stitch over the knitted one can stretch out that stitch, so slip, slip, knit is usually preferred since both stitches are worked into simultaneously, which leaves them closer to the same size.

Knit 2 Together Through the Back Loop (k2tog tbl)

Yet another way to create a decrease is to knit both stitches through their back loops. Rather than work through the front legs of the stitches as normal, insert the needle into the back loops, or legs, of the two stitches and knit them off as one. Unfortunately, this means both stitches are now twisted at their bases. You've now turned both stitches around (page 47), torquing them. This decrease appears in many standard patterns.

Knit 2 together through the back loop

Left-Slanting Decrease

You'll notice how there's only one way to do a right-slanting decrease (k2tog) yet there are several ways of working the left-slanting decrease. And they never quite match; the left-slanting decrease is always looser and sloppier. With all that tugging and manipulating and pulling, of course these stitches will loosen up. And they require extra moves: four for ssk and three for skp. Although k2tog tbl is only one move, the stitches are wonky. These extra moves slow down the work and break up the rhythm. I call it knittus-interruptus.

I have a perfect left-slanting decrease that I guarantee will be the closest match to a right-slanting decrease, and it only requires one move. The one drawback is that you have to prepare for it the row before you do it. We

Preparing for left slanting decrease

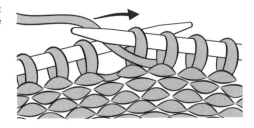

normally like to work our decreases on the right-side (or RS) rows. This means that on the wrong-side (WS) row before you have to do the left-slanting decrease, you also have to know where those two stitches are. It's not too difficult since we tend to work the decrease a stitch or two from the end. Work to those two stitches on the wrong side and insert your needle as if to purl into the first of these; stop. Think about how the yarn normally wraps around the needle in a purl. Go through the motions if you have to. Now wrap the yarn around the needle in the *opposite* direction, going underneath the needle first to the back, then over the top and to the front, and complete the purl.

Repeat this on the next stitch. Purl the remaining stitches normally. When you begin to work the next right-side row, notice that those two stitches are turned the opposite way. They have been primed for you to knit them through their back legs now; they will not twist. That's because they have been preturned from the row before when you purled throwing the opposite way. It's almost as if you've done the slip, slip already for slip, slip, knit (ssk).

EASTERN KNITTING. This way of throwing the purl is not wrong. A lot of Eastern European cultures do it, and it's called Eastern knitting. Some Continental knitters find this path of the purl far easier to work, so it's sometimes known as the lazy purl. However, because the stitches are turned facing the opposite way from normal, these knitters knit into the *back* loops on the following row to prevent twisting or crossing. So its full name is Eastern uncrossed knitting; still others call it Combination knitting. Note that when you throw the opposite direction in purl, you use a bit less yarn. That's why Eastern uncrossed, or Combination, knitters often get shorter row gauges, and it's one of the reasons why this left-slanting decrease is a better match to the right-slanting decrease. The other reason is that there is no extra manipulation to enlarge these stitches.

THROWING THE OPPOSITE WAY FOR KNITTING IN THE ROUND. Just as you can throw the opposite way in purl, you can throw the opposite way in knit as well. When working in the round, there is no wrong-side row; the right side always faces you. To prepare for a left-slanting decrease the row before, identify where the two stitches that will be knitted together for the decrease are. Insert the needle into the stitch as if to knit, then think about how the yarn is normally wrapped and do the opposite. Repeat for the next stitch. On the following round, these preturned stitches facing the opposite way are now ready for knitting through their back loops for a left-slanting decrease. This is a boon for sock knitting because socks are usually worked in the round and, come time to do the toes, you'll love this. If you forget to preturn, you'll have to resort to one of the old-fashioned decrease methods.

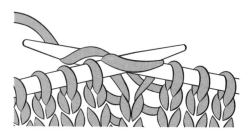

Throwing the opposite way for knitting in the round

Increases

Just as we shape with decreases, so too do we shape with an increase (inc). There are many ways to increase, but let me mention one in particular that I can improve on.

Knit in Front and Back (kf&b)

Known as the bar increase because it produces a horizontal bar in the fabric that resembles a purl, this is easy to do. Knit into the stitch as usual but do *not* remove it from the left-hand needle. Now knit into the *back* loop, or leg, of this same stitch and take the stitch off the needle. This is sometimes aptly called the twice-knit increase.

Knit in front and back

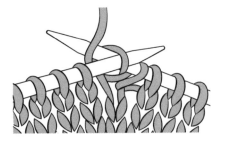

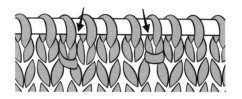

Knitting into
back and front
(left) and front
and back (right)

● **TIP** KNIT IN *BACK* AND *FRONT* OF STITCH

My issue with knitting into the front and back
(kf&b) of a stitch is that on a smooth stockinette surface, the purl-like bump is really
glaring. My solution is to reverse the sequence: Knit into the *back* first, then the
front of the stitch. While this still produces a
bump, it does not stand out as much, and the
bar is a bit more diagonal than horizontal.

● **TIP** KEEPING TRACK OF ROWS

Rather than constantly having to count rows
from the beginning, especially in a long
piece, mark off every ten or twenty rows.
Not only is it helpful to count just from the
last marker, but if this piece is to be
seamed to another piece later, the marked
rows will help you match up the pieces perfectly. You can use either coilless safety
pins, plastic locking stitch markers, scrap
pieces of yarns, or split ring markers—even
bobby pins and paper clips will do.

● **TIP** DELICIOUS KNITTING

From time to time, instructions tell you to do something every so many rows. For instance, in a sleeve, you may have to increase a stitch at either end every fourth row six times, then every sixth row ten times. You can mark this on paper, but pieces of paper tend to get lost. Here's the method my friend Claire Gregorcyk of Atlanta has for counting rows. She lays out as many little chocolate candies (she likes to use M&M's™) as there are rows until the next instruction. Once the candy is finished, she works the increase or decrease or color change and lays out another four or six candies or whatever number is needed. While not recommended for the diabetic, this trick does give you incentive to work faster. For those of us who are more diet conscious, peanuts or raisins work as well. Just make sure the dog and the kids are not around.

Seriously, it's also a good idea to mark the row where you've worked your increase or your decrease. That way, not only can you count the rows more easily, you can see how many increases or decreases have been worked just by looking for the marker. You can even use one color marker for one set of instructions (such as the "every four rows") and another color for the other set (such as the "every six rows").

● **TIP** SLOPING A SHOULDER

In garments, having sloping shoulders is a good idea since that's the way most bodies are shaped. If your instructions do not call for this, you can easily make a sloping seam. Work your armholes 1 inch (2.5cm) longer than directed. When putting the sweater together, use my cheat method: Stitch the shoulder seam with a slanted straight line, starting about 1 inch (2.5cm) down from the top at the outer shoulder and tapering upward toward the neck, ending at the top of the piece at the neck. This seam creates a bit more bulk and may be visible through lacier stitches, but its ease in working offsets these minor issues. Either machine-sew or backstitch by hand the diagonal line with the right sides facing each other. Separate the extra fabric near the arms and tack it down on the wrong side to form mini shoulder pads.

When instructions do call for shoulder shaping, it usually involves having to bind off a series of stitches forming ungainly stair steps, which are hard to seam later. Now you can work the shoulders straight instead and then sew the pieces together with the sloping shoulder seam. This is especially useful when you do not want to shape the shoulders while working an intricate stitch pattern at the same time.

Sewing a sloping shoulder seam

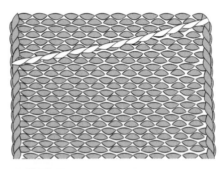

Fold back excess and tack down

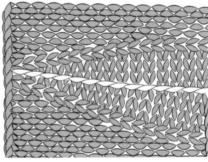

Finished slanted seam

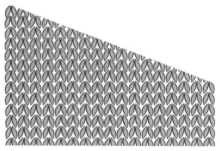

Fixing Mistakes

∙ ∙

Mistakes are inevitable. Who among us is
perfect? Indeed, some cultures put a mistake
into their works, on purpose because they
believe only God is perfect. I say mistakes
will happen naturally enough so you don't
have to go out of your way to put one in.

Duplicate Stitch

The duplicate stitch, also known as Swiss
darning, follows the path of the stitch with a
separate strand of yarn threaded into a
darning needle. It's typically used for adding
some color after the knitting is complete,
and it is simpler than intarsia. It's so
versatile; it can even be used to correct
mistakes. I like to call it the "dupe" stitch, as
that implies fooling or tricking someone,
as in being duped! Eventually, you will come
across the term Kitchener stitch or graft

when you have to invisibly sew tops of stitches together, as in the toes of socks. This is nothing but a variation of duplicate stitch. Instead of working over existing stitches, you are creating new stitches with yarn and darning needle. It's used to mend torn knitting as well.

Using duplicate stitch to fix knit to purl

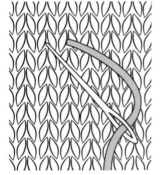

● **TIP** DUPLICATE STITCH TO FIX KNIT TO PURL
You knitted a stitch when it should have been purled. Thread your yarn onto a yarn needle and darn horizontally across the offending knit stitch by bringing the needle up on one side of the stitch from back to front, then inserting the needle into other side of the stitch from front to back. Weave in the ends. Compare the real purl to this fixed phony purl. It's not perfect, but it's close enough. If someone notices the difference, they're way too close!

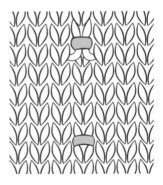

Real purl (top) and fixed purl (bottom)

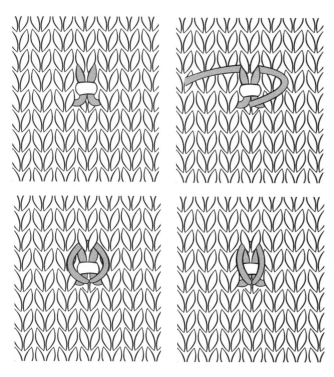

Duplicate stitch
over a purl

● **TIP** DUPLICATE STITCH TO FIX PURL TO KNIT

You purled a stitch that should have been
knitted. This is a bit trickier. Again, thread
your yarn onto a yarn needle. Insert the needle at the base of the purl stitch from back to
front below the mistake, then insert the
needle behind the middle of the stitch horizontally from front to back to front, and end
by going back into the base of the purl stitch
where you began. Compare the real knit to

this fixed knit. Again, it's not perfect, but it's a whole lot better than ripping out.

If you're still bothered by that small, little blip, work yet another one of these duplicate stitches directly above the one you just made.

● **TIP** DUPLICATE STITCH TO FIX A WRONGLY CROSSED CABLE

Okay, now you've done it. You messed up a cable quite a ways back by accidentally crossing it the wrong way, and it's glaring. Rather than rip out all your hard work, use duplicate stitch to fix it. Here are left-cross cables at the bottom and top, but a right-cross in the center. These are four-stitch cables, or two stitches crossed over two stitches. With yarn threaded on to the needle, duplicate stitch diagonally over the offending middle cross. Begin with the first stitch *below* the cable and work up and around the third stitch *above* the cable.

Shove stitches aside and pull the cable apart to really find the stitches. For the second stitch, come up through the second

Wrongly
crossed cables

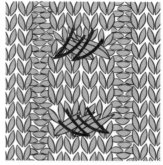

Fixing left to right (top)
and right to left (bottom)

stitch below the cable and go around the
fourth stitch above the cable. On larger
cables such as a six-stitch cable (three
crossed over three), the first stitch below
goes to the fourth stitch above, the second
one below to the fifth above; and the third
below stitch to the sixth above. Can you figure out an eight-stitch cable? To fix a left-
cross to a right-cross in our four-stitcher,
you go from third stitch below to first above,
fourth stitch below to second above.

Fixed cables

Dropping Stitches to Fix a Cable

If you haven't worked far after "miscrossing" a cable, you can fix it by dropping the stitches and reknitting them. You use a crochet hook to "ladder" the stitches back up. Think of it as creating a run in your stocking on purpose. I know, I hear that loud gulp. It's not so bad. Try it on a swatch first. Drop one stitch intentionally and let it run a few rows down; in most cases you'll find that you have to force it to run. Pick up the last fully formed stitch with the crochet hook from front to back (without twisting it), *lay the next loose strand on the hook and pull through. Repeat from *. It's like forming a crocheted chain.

With cables you will be dropping more than this one stitch. The good news is that for a simple cable, you only have to drop *half* the cable—the last cable crossed left rather than right.

Laddering up dropped stitches

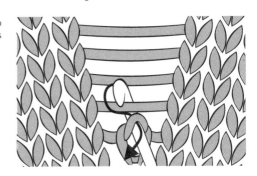

Dropping stitches to fix a cable

1. A miscrossed cable

2. Dropping the cable stitches

3. Bringing dropped stitches to the other side

4. Laddering up

5. The fixed cable

You can drop the first two stitches or the last two—either way works—but choosing the half that should end up on top of the cable will be easier to do. Unravel only to the row below the crossing and place both stitches onto a coilless safety pin or a locking stitch marker. On a larger cable such as, a six-stitch, you drop three stitches for half the cable, and on an eight-stitch, you would drop four stitches.

Now push those two stitches to the *opposite* side of the fabric. (These were in back, so I brought them to the front.)

Use a crochet hook to ladder up each stitch, one at a time. Of course, if you wanted to make a cable cross in the other direction, you'd bring these stitches from the front to the back. If the cable were bigger, such as a six-stitch, you would drop three stitches for half the cable, and for an eight-stitch, you'd drop four stitches.

● **TIP** USING FELT-TIP MARKERS FOR COLOR

I once made a mistake while knitting a two-color Fair Isle pattern, working a white stitch where a black one should have been. Not wanting to rip out the two strands, I could have worked a duplicate stitch over the offending stitch. Instead, I did the down-and-dirty felt-tip marker trick. Don't be so shocked. Sharpies™ are great. They are available at fabric or quilting stores; come in a variety of colors; and are *permanent*, which is the key to using them on knitted fabric.

If you don't know how to knit with two colors across the row, often referred to as Fair Isle, color in your stitches with permanent magic marker instead. You may not want to do a whole lot of it, but a scattered faux lice pattern (found in classic Scandinavian designs) of dark dots on light yarn works well. The resulting fabric will be less bulky, and your fingers won't get caught in the stranded floats on the back. Work very carefully as you saturate each stitch fully and then allow ample time for the fabric to dry.

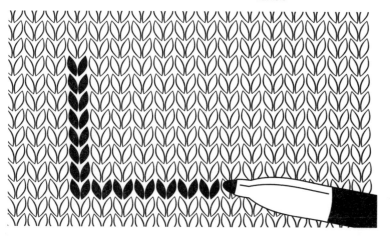

Using felt-tip markers

5

In This Chapter

148 **Binding Off**

148 Crochet Hook Bind-Off in Knit

150 Crochet Hook Bind-Off in Purl

151 Three-Needle Bind-Off

152 Two-Needles-and-a-Hook Bind-Off

152 Decrease Bind-Off

156 **Blocking**

162 **Seaming**

163 Whipstitch

164 Back Stitch

165 Slip Stitch

166 Single Crochet

167 Mattress Stitch

172 **Joining as You Go**

177 Seam-as-You-Go Cardigan

178 **Setting in Drop-Shoulder Sleeves**

180 Picking Up Stitches Evenly

181 Pick Up *as if* to Knit

184 **Spacing Buttons Evenly**

186 **Making Buttonholes**

189 Making Buttonholes in a Garter Stitch Band

190 Sewing on Buttons

191 Knitting on Buttons

195 **Weaving in Ends**

197 Using a Latch Hook

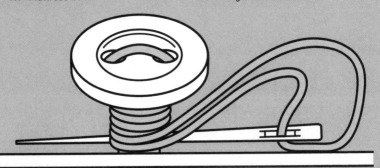

Finishing

It's now time to **tackle** that dreaded "f" word. (No, not *that* one.) Most knitters I know despise the finishing process. When the knitting is done, they want it to be done. I like to quote one of my all-time favorite baseball heroes, Yogi Berra. **It ain't over till it's over.**

Binding Off

. . . .

You're at the end of your project at last, and you're ecstatic. You're ready to bind off. My guess is that the process of binding off is not one of your favorites; it certainly isn't mine. I hate that "passing the first stitch over the second" business. And the bind-offs are invariably way too tight, even if you go up a needle size or two. It's the tugging action when you pass that first stitch over the second that tightens the work. Try substituting a crochet hook for a knitting needle.

Crochet Hook Bind-Off in Knit

Use a crochet hook about the same size as your needle (page 101) because you'll be knitting with the crochet hook. Insert the hook into the first stitch, wrap the yarn around the hook (you can actually hold the yarn in the left hand as if crocheting), draw the yarn through, and take the stitch off. You've now knitted the first stitch with the hook. *Insert the hook into the next stitch, yarn around the hook, pull this yarn through both the stitch on the needle and the loop on the hook, and take the stitch off the left-hand needle. You've now bound off the first stitch. There is one stitch left on your hook.

Repeat from * until all stitches are bound off; fasten and end off. In essence, this technique is the same as a knitted bind-off. Instead of passing the first stitch over the second, you are *pulling the second stitch under the first*, which produces the same results. Not only will you find this faster and easier, the bound-off edge will never be too tight. In fact, it may be too loose. Here, using a crochet hook a size larger or smaller will affect the tension of the bind-off, so adjust accordingly.

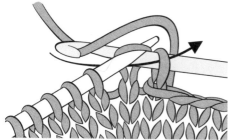

Crochet hook
bind-off in knit

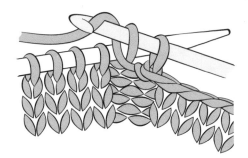

Crochet hook
bind-off in purl

Crochet Hook Bind-Off in Purl

Directions often tell you to bind off in pattern. Just as you can knit with a hook, so too can you purl with a hook. To bind off in purl, bring the yarn to the front, ready to purl. Insert the hook as if to purl from back to front, grab the yarn, and pull it through the stitch and the loop on the hook. I find rotating the hook away from me helps push it in a purlwise fashion. I then rotate the hook again to get the loop through the one on the hook. Purling is a bit trickier but doable; it just requires a little bit of practice.

Three-Needle Bind-Off

For a three-needle bind-off, join the pieces
with right sides facing and with the needles
aligned and both points facing right. Insert

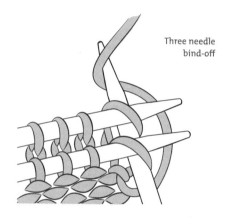

Three needle
bind-off

a third needle (hence the name) into the first
stitch of the front needle and into the
first stitch of the back needle and knit them
together.

There will be one stitch left on your
right-hand needle. *Insert the third needle
into the next stitch on the front needle
and the next stitch on the back needle and
knit these two stitches together. Pass the
first stitch on the right-hand needle over the
second to bind off. Repeat from * until all
stitches are bound off; fasten and end off.

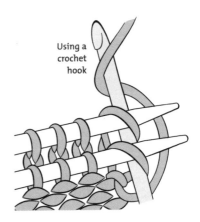

Using a crochet hook

Two-Needles-and-a-Hook Bind-Off

With the three-needle bind-off, I don't mind
the two needles in my left hand, but I do
mind having to use the tip of one of them to
lift one stitch over the other. So instead
I use a two-needle-and-a-crochet-hook
bind-off. You work as you would the
crocheted bind-off (page 150) but insert the
hook through one stitch on each of the
two needles and pull through both stitches
and the loop on the hook.

Decrease Bind-Off

If you don't have a crochet hook handy, you
can use the decrease (k2tog) bind-off. Knit
the first two stitches together through their
back loops. Now take the stitch on the
right-hand needle and place it back onto the

left-hand needle. *Knit the next two stitches together through their back loops. Take the stitch on the right-hand needle and place it back onto the left-hand needle. Repeat from * until the last two stitches are knitted together. Fasten and end off. If you knit the two stitches together like a regular knit stitch, you would get little vertical bars. By knitting them together through their back loops, you create a chain across the top that looks like a regular bind-off.

To bind off in pattern with the decrease method, knit two stitches together through the back loops above the knit stitches and purl two together in the usual way above the purl stitches. Place the yarn to the front to prepare to purl before placing the knit stitch back onto the left-hand needle, and place the yarn to the back to prepare to knit before placing the purl stitch back onto the left-hand needle.

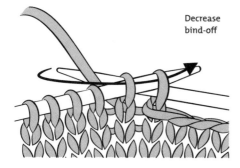

Decrease
bind-off

● **TIP** COMPLETING THE CIRCULAR BIND-OFF

When binding off on circular knitting (again, I prefer the term "spiral"), you'll see how the last stitch is high and the next one to its left is low. This happens on all circular knitting, but when it's at the neckband, it's most noticeable.

Why is there a gap between the last stitch and the first stitch? All other stitches have a solid chain over them from the bind-off, which really begins after the first stitch and ends at the last stitch, leaving that space between the first and last stitches with no chain from a bind-off over it. My solution is to bind off until there is that last loop on your right-hand needle, or hook. Clip the yarn, leaving a 6-inch (15cm) tail, then pull up on that needle or hook's last loop until it comes undone and the tail pops out. Thread this tail onto a yarn needle.

At the base of the tail is the last bind-off chain. Use the tail to create a duplicate stitch—a false chain stitch—to join this last stitch to the first. The first bind-off chain is to the left and above the first stitch, between the first and second stitches. Insert the needle underneath both legs of this first bind-off chain. Pull the yarn through and insert the needle down into the last bind-off chain, the same one that the tail popped

Completing the circular bind-off

The space between
first and last stitches

Pulling up on
last loop

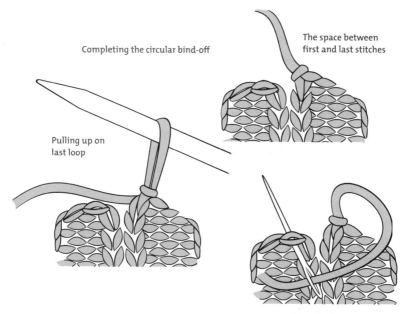

out of; pull the needle through, adjusting
the tension so that the duplicate stitch is the
same size as the other chains in the bind-off
and leaving the remainder of the tail behind
the work to be woven in. Except for the tail,
you can't tell the beginning from the end
anymore. Is this a smooth finish or what?

You can use this technique to join the gap
at the beginning cast-on of any circularly
knit piece using the tail from the cast-on. It
may not be as neat and tidy because there
may not be chains there, depending on how
you cast on; but it does close the gap.

Creating a duplicate
chain stitch

The improved
bind-off

Blocking

I prefer to block before seaming pieces together, although I sometimes steam the seams flat after seaming as well. Blocking is so underrated; I'm rather shocked at how few knitters actually do it. I know, it's that extra step, but just look at what it can do: The swatch on the left was steam blocked, and the one on the right was not. Notice that knitting in its raw state, especially stockinette, has a tendency to curl. The sides curl away from you, and the top and bottom edges curl toward you. Knitters often ask how to fix this. Short of sticking the offending piece under a mattress for a week (and even that won't be a permanent fix), I highly recommend steam blocking, even for synthetics.

Steam provides heat as well as moisture, and it's the heat that sets a piece, so it's important to use a really good steam iron. I actually have a floor steamer that looks like a vacuum cleaner hose connected to a water cooler. There's no metal to get hot, so there's no chance of scorching. These steamers tend to be pricy, but they are so multipurpose that I find it worthwhile. My husband gets the wrinkles out of his shirt in the morning, a friend borrowed it to remove old wallpaper, and I use it for facials. Well worth the investment.

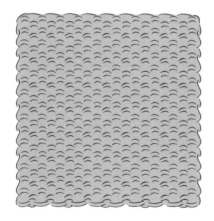

Steam-blocked swatch

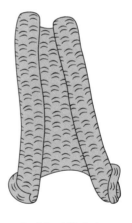

Swatch not blocked

BLOCKING THE SWATCH FIRST. Try blocking, especially steaming, the swatch first. Steaming takes out any irregularities in your stitching, making it look better; but it can also relax your the knitting. You want to make sure that the results after steaming will still match your gauge. I often knit slightly tighter than normal to make sure I get the gauge after steam blocking. When directions tell you to "block pieces to measurements," this is what they mean. After steaming, wool may lose a bit of its spring and loft as it softens. Steaming can add more slink to rayon or silk. To steam acrylic, use a good steam iron without ever touching the hot iron to the fabric, and move the iron around constantly, not hovering over any one spot for long. Allow the piece to dry thoroughly. I recommend that you do some testing on a few swatches, comparing steamed and nonsteamed pieces of the same swatches.

"KILLING A FABRIC." This is an industry term that means you can very carefully press the fabric with a hot iron. This changes the look, feel, drape, body, and texture forever. Whether this is good or bad depends on the project and the individual knitter. Many knitters like the dressier sheen and drape on garments that have been pressed. A bonus is that once "killed," the stitches are set for life (I know, a bit of a contradiction here) and the fabric is stabilized. It will not grow any longer, or shrink any further. The gauge after killing should match the pattern's gauge. You can iron synthetics, too, but always place a pressing cloth over the project to avoid a sticky iron.

Some knitters like spring and loft in a fabric, such as in a baby afghan, so just wet-block those projects. Let the project determine whether killing is appropriate or not; and always do it on the swatch first, especially when killing can radically alter your stitch gauge. Proceed cautiously since, as in real life, once killed, there's no resurrection.

THE EQUIPMENT. I like a good blocking board, and I have several. You can make one yourself using plywood and gingham fabric with one-inch squares. Lay some batting or an old blanket on the board, cover with the fabric, and staple all around. Some knitters have great success using a foam board. It's become popular to use children's rubber jigsaw puzzle flooring pieces for blocking, but if there's heat involved (as in steaming), I'd think twice about doing this and ending up with melted goo.

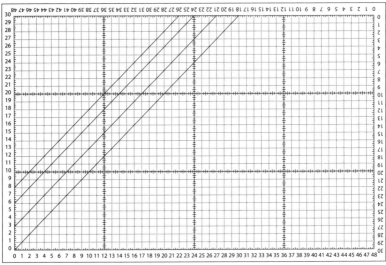

Blocking board
and T-pins

After washing and rinsing, lay the piece on a towel to soak up the moisture. If the piece is small enough, use a salad spinner; it removes the water and is less messy. For a larger piece, use as many towels as you need to absorb the water, then lay out the piece to measurement on the blocking board. Secure the piece with pins every inch or so or use blocking wires, which I prefer. You insert these flexible, stainless steel wires through all the edges and ease the pieces out like a kite to size. I find using wires prevents the scalloping along the edges that usually happens when using pins. For seamless garments in the round, you can use the wires where the seams would be. If you don't have a blocking board with a grid, you can use a tape measure to lay out the pieces to size, then steam them and let them dry.

The beauty of blocking before seaming is that the edges lie flat, and that makes seaming easier. It's also easier to block the pieces individually. After assembling, I steam the seams for a really polished look.

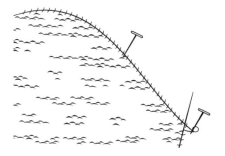

Blocking wires
and T-pins

Seaming

Don't all groan at the same time. If done
well, a seam can be a thing of beauty. There
are several ways to sew up things, and you
can even piece things together without any
sewing. Note that all these methods can be
used either for side seams or, top and bottom seams, and even on curved seams such
as armholes and sleeve caps. Many knitters
like to pin or baste their pieces together
before seaming, and that is why it's important
to mark off every so many rows (page 00).
These markers will help you match equal
portions of each piece.

● **TIP** STARTING WITH A SLIP KNOT

**If you did not reel off seaming yarn at the be-
ginning of the project, you will have to attach
new yarn now. You have to anchor
the new yarn; if not, it can pop out as
you are sewing. I like to attach it with
the slip knot. Make a slip knot in the
tail yarn, insert the needle into the
fabric, then insert the needle
through the slip knot before you
tighten. Pulling through and tightening closes up the slip knot.**

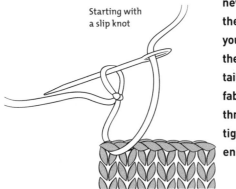

Starting with
a slip knot

● **TIP** ENDING WITH A FRENCH KNOT

I like to end any sewn seams with a French knot. To do this, wrap the yarn around the top of the needle a few times before inserting it into the last stitch. Pull to close tight.

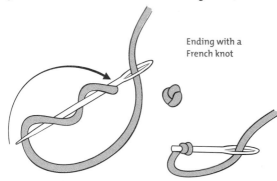

Ending with a French knot

Whipstitch

The whipstitch, or overcast stitch, is one of the easiest and most common seams, and it was probably one of the very first seams I did. To make this seam, place the pieces with right sides together and bring the needle from back to front (or vice versa) under both strands of a stitch on each piece, then over both stitches. Continue along the length of the seam. This is a relatively bulk-free seam, good to use with thicker yarn and textured yarns, where it's difficult to see individual stitches. It's flexible; good for garments but not for projects such as purses, which are not meant to stretch.

The whipstitch seam

Back Stitch

Backstitching creates a strong and firm seam, great for shoulders. It is a bit bulky, however, so use it for worsted-weight yarns and thinner. Place the pieces with right sides facing together. Think of backstitching as being, somewhat like the bunny hop, but here it's two steps forward and one step back. More precisely, start from the right edge of the fabric with the needle going from front to back through both fabrics; call this point A. Move to the left and insert the needle from back to front; call this point C. Insert the needle halfway between A and C from front to back; this is point B. Move to the left beyond C and insert the needle from back to front; this is point D. Now come front to back through point C and then from back to front at point E. Continue this way: in through D and out through F, in through E and out through G, along the entire seam.

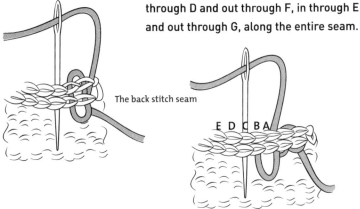

The back stitch seam

E D C B A

Slip Stitch

As a crocheter, I like the slip stitch seam, which is crocheting, not sewing. Once again, have the right sides facing each other. Begin with a slip knot on the hook and *insert the hook through both fabrics from front to back, yarn around the hook, and pull through both fabrics and the loop on the hook. Repeat from *. This is a sturdy, nonstretchy seam, good for coats and jackets and handbags. It is quite bulky, however, so I would not recommend it for heavier yarns. The beauty of the slip stitch is that it is easily taken out should you make a mistake. It's also terrific for novelty yarns, where it's difficult to see individual stitches. For most seams, I recommend going into both loops of the stitch, but with slip stitching that creates extra bulk, so I just work into one loop of the stitch.

The slip stitch seam

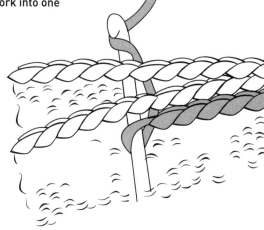

Single Crochet

Similar to the slip stitch seam, the single crochet seam is typically worked into one loop only. This seam can be worked on the right side of the fabric, forming a decorative seam. Place the pieces with wrong sides together for a decorative seam, right sides together for a nonvisible seam. Begin with a slip knot on the hook and *insert the hook through one loop of each fabric, yarn around the hook, and pull through a loop. Yarn over and pull through both loops on the hook. Repeat from *. This is bulkier than slip stitch and slightly stretchier. It can be ripped out quite easily, and it's terrific for novelty yarns.

The single crochet seam

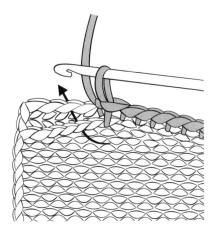

Mattress Stitch

Contrary to its name, mattress seaming
does not require sewing in bed. I'm not
certain how it got its name, perhaps because
it lies flat, but it is my all-time favorite seam.
I find it the most invisible and the least bulky.
And since you seam with the right sides facing you, you can always see what it looks like
as you're doing it. The one drawback is that
it is very precise, so there is little room for
error. The number of rows on each side must
match exactly. Let me state again the impor-
tance of marking off every so many rows as
described on page 133. In mattress seaming,
you're looking for the strand of yarn *between*
the edge stitch and the next stitch in.

THE BASIC MATTRESS SEAM. Begin with the
pieces abutting each other. Thread the yarn
onto a yarn needle; if you have not reserved
seaming yarn from the cast-on, start with
the slip knot (page 41) and join the cast-on
edge of one piece to the cast-on edge of the
other piece. Insert the needle back into the
first cast-on edge again and tighten. Now
insert the needle from front to back under
two strands on one piece, then under two
strands on the other piece, and tighten.
Always insert the needle in a continuous
motion down under the first strand and then

The basic
mattress
seam

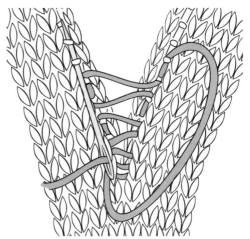

back out above the second before tightening.
Continue in this way for the entire seam.

SEAMING STRIPES. To be more precise, as you
line up stripes, the rows have to be offset
and not directly in line with one another.

I'll refer to the rows of one piece (A) as 1A,
2A, 3A, and so on, and the rows of the other
piece (B) as 1B, 2B, 3B, and so on. Try this
out on striped swatches so that you can
clearly distinguish the rows.

For either reserved seaming yarn or for joined seaming yarn, thread a yarn needle and go from one piece (A) to the other piece (B) and insert the needle from back to front of the bottom cast-on edge of B.

Insert the needle from back to front of the cast-on edge of A again, and tighten.

Now insert needle from front to back of the bottom end chain of B and then in a continuing motion, from back to front of the end stitch of row 1B, and tighten.

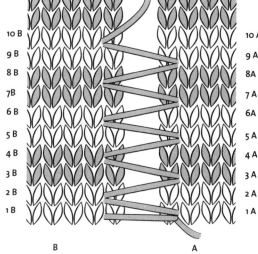

Seaming stripes

10 B   10 A
9 B   9 A
8 B   8A
7B   7 A
6 B   6A
5 B   5 A
4 B   4 A
3 B   3 A
2 B   2 A
1 B   1 A

B   A

Insert the needle from front to back of the end stitch of row 1A and then in a continuing motion, from back to front of the end stitch of row 2A, and tighten.

Always insert the needle in a continuous motion down through the first part and then back out the second part before tightening.

Now insert the needle from front to back of the end stitch of row 1B and then from back to front of the end stitch of row 3B, and tighten.

Tightening the yarn as you go

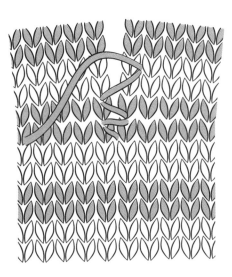

Insert the needle from front to back of the end stitch of row 2A and then from back to front of the end stitch of row 4A, and tighten.

Insert the needle from front to back of the end stitch of row 3B and then from back to front of the end stitch of row 5B, and tighten.

Insert the needle from front to back of the end stitch of row 4A and then from back to front of the end stitch of row 6A, and tighten.

Insert the needle from front to back of the end stitch of row 5B and then from back to front of end stitch of row 7B, and tighten. Are you getting the idea? The rows are off-set. After the initial join and setup, go through the *even* rows on one side and the *odd* rows in the other. This is most important when trying to match patterns such as stripes.

If done right, the join is practically invisible. This is why tightening is important. Too tight, however, and the seam puckers. Pull on the seam itself every so often to avoid this. At the end, work the French knot (page 163) with the needle going through both thicknesses at the top. Notice how the end stitches of each side roll to the back. While not totally bulk-free, mattress seaming can be used for just about anything.

Joining as You Go

• •

Believe it or not, it is possible to knit a new piece and attach it to an existing one at the same time! Not only is there no seaming afterward, this join is quite imperceptible and has very little bulk. Of course, there are disadvantages as well. If you make a mistake, it entails having to rip out a lot of your work.

JOINING A NEW PIECE ON THE RIGHT. To work on a new piece that will wind up on the right of the old piece, have the right side facing.

Reel off a tail at least three times the length of the edge on which you're working. With a circular or long double-pointed needle, pick up every other row with the tail yarn that you just reeled off (more on picking up later).
Go back to the beginning where the working yarn is and cast on the stitches for the new piece at the beginning of the circular or double-pointed needle.

With a separate needle, knit the new piece to the last stitch; *knit the next two stitches together through the back loops (eliminating one picked-up stitch).

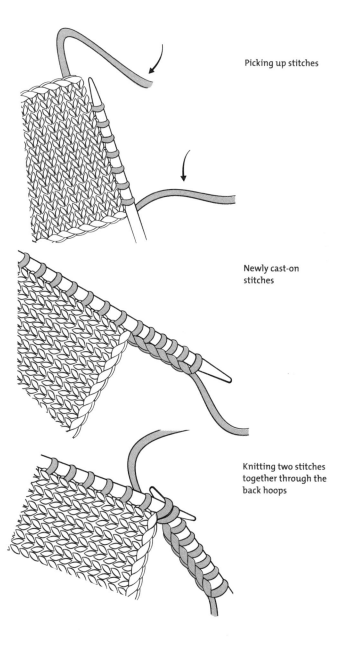

Picking up stitches

Newly cast-on
stitches

Knitting two stitches
together through the
back hoops

A new piece
joined on the
right

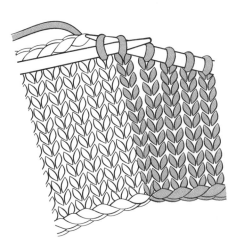

Turn, using the circular or double-pointed
needle as your right-hand needle, slip the
first stitch as if to purl, and continue to work
the wrong side of the new piece.

Repeat from * until all picked-up stitches
have been knit into the new piece.

Note that each picked-up stitch corresponds
to *two* rows of new knitting (which is why you
picked up a stitch every other row). A smooth
slip stitch chain is created at the "seam."

JOINING A NEW PIECE ON THE LEFT. To join
the opposite, or left, edge of an exiting piece,
there is no need to reel off a tail. Just pick

up every other row from top to bottom with right side facing and then use the same yarn to cast on for your new piece. On wrong-side rows, you attach the new piece to the old piece at the last stitch by purling the last stitch together with the next picked-up stitch. On right-side rows, you slip the first stitch as if to purl while leaving the yarn at the back.

OTHER USES. This technique can be used to attach edgings, too; but in order to pick up every other row, the row gauge of the new piece must match that of the old piece. If it does not, you will get a ruffled effect.

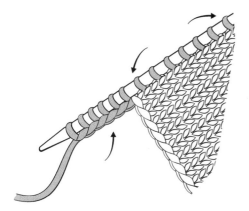

Joining a new
piece on the left

This technique can be used if the row gauge of the new piece doesn't match that of the old piece, but both pieces will be the same height. In this case, determine ahead of time the row gauge of the trim or new piece by swatching it. Figure out how many total rows are necessary to trim or add to the given edge using the trim's row gauge. Pick up *half* the number of rows along that edge. If you know you need one hundred rows to trim a side edge, pick up fifty stitches evenly along that side edge (page 000). For example, if the trim has one hundred rows in 20 inches (51cm) and the body has eighty rows in 20 inches (51cm), you can't pick up every other row, because the rows don't match. If you pick up fifty stitches (half of one hundred) to attach to the eighty rows of the existing piece—the body—you will be picking up five stitches for every eight rows. To do this, you pick up two stitches, skip one, pick up three stitches, skip one, pick up two stitches, and so on across the row.

Seam-as-You-Go Cardigan

This type of join looks so good and invisible that even when it's worked in a different color, there is a continuity of fabric. I'd even use this method instead of working traditional intarsia (page 121) on a sweater that is half one color and half another. When making a garment, this means you can work the left front of a cardigan first, then work the back by joining it to the left front, then work the right front by joining it to the back, and not have to work the side seams. You can even join the front of a sweater to the back as you knit it by joining at each end every other row.

Seam-as-you-go
cardigan

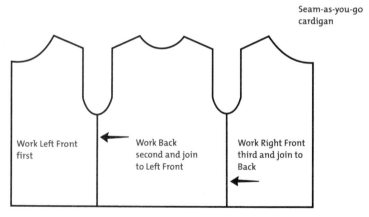

Work Left Front first

Work Back second and join to Left Front

Work Right Front third and join to Back

Setting in Drop-Shoulder Sleeves

When sewing the sleeves to the body in a simple, drop-shoulder garment, the stitches at the top of the sleeves will be joined to the rows of the body. Remember: The stitch gauge is not the same as the row gauge; stitches are short and wide. So when sewing sleeve stitches into body rows, you will have to skip an occasional row. The problem is that the pieces are not always perfectly matched.

● **TIP** PICKING UP STITCHES FROM THE ARMHOLE FIRST

I have an easier way to set in a sleeve. First, do *not* bind off the stitches at the top of the sleeves. Leave them on a needle, a stitch holder, or a piece of yarn waste. Pick up the same number of stitches around the armhole as there are stitches at the top of the sleeves. You can use the same working yarn as the last row of the sleeve knitting to pick up with so you don't have extra ends to weave in.

For example, let's say there are 103 stitches at the top of the sleeve. After joining the shoulder seam, mark off the front and back armhole and divide it into sections. Pick up 103 stitches along this marked armhole. There are now exactly the same number of stitches along the rows of this armhole, and each one of these stitches can now be joined to a stitch of the sleeve. Use the three-needle bind-off or the two-needles-and-a-hook bind-off. Heck, I'd even use the same working yarn as the last row of the sleeve knitting to pick up the stitches along the armhole. Why have extra ends to weave in? With a one-to-one correspondence of stitches picked up from the body to stitches picked up from the sleeve, you can now turn off your brain and stop counting all the time.

Joining the sleeve to the armhole

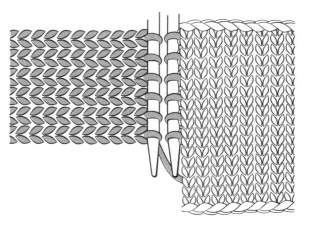

Picking Up Stitches Evenly

The directions say "pick up and knit 103 stitches evenly along side edge" and you gulp. That edge is so long and daunting. I say divide and conquer—break up that long edge into smaller chunks. To do that, fold it in half and mark the halfway point with a plastic locking stitch marker or tie on a piece of scrap yarn. You now have two equal chunks. Fold both in half and mark them; you now have four equal sections. Fold both in half yet again and mark them, and you now have eight equal sections.

Now take the number of stitches and divide by the number of equal sections. That would be 103 ÷ 8 = 13, minus one. You see, 8 x 13 = 104, which is one more than you need. So, between each of the seven markers pick up 13 stitches, except in one section pick up only 12. The nice thing about this method is that, when we suffer from knittus-interruptus, we only have to count from the last marker.

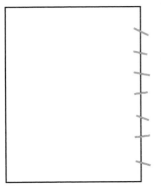

Evenly dividing
an edge to be
trimmed

Another way to divide an edge into equal chunks is by measuring. If the edge is 21inches (53.5cm) long, place a marker every 3 inches (7.5cm) to get seven equal chunks. So 103 ÷ 7 = 15, minus 2. Since 7 x 15 = 105, that's 2 more than you need. Between each of the markers, pick up and knit 15 stitches, except in two sections where you'll pick up only 14 stitches in each.

With either method, the phone can ring, someone can knock on the door, the kids can come in screaming, and the dog can bark at you, maybe all at once. You can still easily find where you have left off and not have to do all that counting again.

Pick Up *as if* to Knit

When directions say to pick up and knit, I think it really should say to pick up *as if* to knit. That is, with the right side facing, insert the needle into the fabric from front to back as if you are going into a stitch knitwise, wrap the yarn around the needle in a knitwise fashion, and bring a loop of the yarn through to the front as if knitting through a stitch. I like to go into the space between the edge stitch, or selvedge, and the next stitch in.

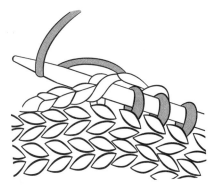

Picking up as if to knit

● **TIP** PICKING UP WITH RIGHT SIDE FACING

We normally pick up with the right side facing, and that means that after the pick-up, the first row is a wrong-side row. Suppose you wanted to establish a complex stitch pattern and you would prefer working the row after the pick-up as a right-side row. Take a cue from Join as You Go (page 172) and pick up using a reeled-off tail of yarn at least three times the length of the edge you're picking up from, and use a circular knitting needle or long double-pointed ones. After you pick up the stitches, without turning, slide the stitches back to the beginning of the pick-up where the ball of yarn is, and begin the first row with the right side still facing you.

● **TIP** A SLIP KNOT FOR THE INITIAL PICK-UP STITCH

When picking up the first stitch, just as when joining a new yarn, the first stitch is loose and sloppy, with nothing holding it down. I have two ways to fix this. One way to alleviate this looseness is to make a slip knot with the yarn, insert the needle, place the slip knot onto the needle, and bring the slip knot through as the first stitch. Make sure to keep the knot to the back of the work, and continue to pick up the rest of the stitches as usual.

If this slip knot really bothers you, begin with the slip knot already on your needle and then pick up the required number of stitches. Do not count the slip knot; it's just there to keep things tight and tidy. On the following row, just take out the slip knot and weave in the end.

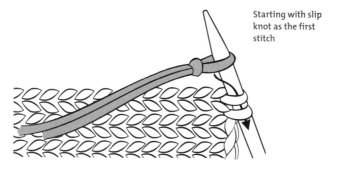

Starting with slip knot as the first stitch

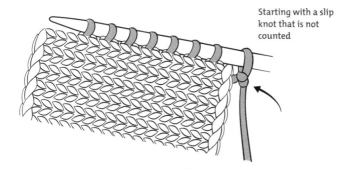

Starting with a slip knot that is not counted

Spacing Buttons Evenly

When it's time to make the button and buttonhole bands on a cardigan, the instructions may say something confounding like "place seven $5/8$-inch (16mm) buttons evenly spaced along the button band, with the top button $1/4$ inch (6mm) from the top edge and the bottom button $2^1/2$ inches (6.5cm) from the bottom edge." How frustrating. But I've got an idea.

Take a piece of white elastic, about $1/2$– 1 inch (13mm–2.5cm) wide and about 12 inches (30.5cm) long. Lay it down flat and draw big dots with a felt-tip marker every inch. These markings represent the number of potential buttons you'll be using, but the markings will not stay 1 inch (2.5cm) apart for long. Choose the number of dots to represent the number of buttons that you will be placing on the cardigan or jacket. Fasten down the elastic so the top dot is $1/4$ inch (6mm) from the top edge, and then pull on the elastic until the bottom dot is $2^1/2$ inches (6.5cm) from the bottom edge. Insert straight pins to mark the spots—you can replace them later with a stitch marker or scrap yarn. You may need an extra pair of hands to help you do this.

There are expandable, trivetlike devices, available from sewing suppliers that evenly space things for you, but the elastic is handy and inexpensive and can be used for other projects such as evenly spacing decorations across a pillow.

Using elastic to space buttons evenly

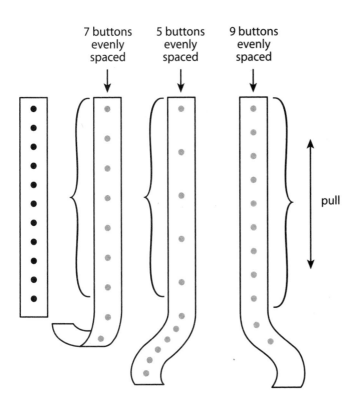

7 buttons evenly spaced

5 buttons evenly spaced

9 buttons evenly spaced

pull

Making Buttonholes

Now that you've evenly spaced the buttons, you need to make buttonholes. How? I say keep it simple. The basic eyelet buttonhole (yarn over, knit 2 together) on page 187 is fine for most buttons. The eyelet hole is one stitch wide—the minimum size. At a typical gauge of four stitches per inch, the eyelet buttonhole is $1/4$ inch (6mm) wide. Two stitches make it $1/2$ inch (13mm) wide. Most buttons for garments are $3/8$ inch (10mm), $1/2$ inch (13mm), or $5/8$ inch (16mm). The thinner your yarn, the smaller the button you'll want to use and vice versa. Using this one-stitch eyelet hole helps keep the size of the buttons and buttonholes in scale with the yarn.

To practice making a buttonhole, cast on a few stitches and work a knit 1, purl 1 ribbing. Button bands are usually knit in ribbing or some other noncurling stitch.

The loose strands of a yarn-over buttonhole

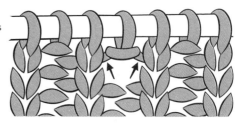

After a few rows, work up to a buttonhole row, preferably a right-side row. Notice that in ribbing, the knit stitches stand out and the purl stitches recede. Place the buttonholes in the purl recesses.

Row 1 (right side): *Work up to a purl stitch where you want to place the buttonhole, yarn over, knit 2 together; repeat from *.
Row 2: Work in rib pattern as established.

For years, this was the only buttonhole I made because, well, it was the only one I knew. It worked well enough, but the top of the hole has these strands of yarn cascading down and I've caught these swags many times trying to push a slightly larger button through.

● **TIP** A PERFECT BUTTONHOLE
To reinforce an eyelet buttonhole and tighten those swags, after rows 1 and 2 work this row next:
Row 3: *Work ribbing to the purl stitch above the yarn-over eyelet and purl into the yarn-over eyelet instead of into the purl stitch over it, and drop the stitch just above it; repeat from *.

Instead of working into the purl stitch on the needle, you insert the needle into the honking-big yarn-over hole as if to purl (or from back to front). The hole is huge; you can't miss it! Wrap the yarn purlwise and purl it through the yarn-over hole, then drop the stitch that's directly above the yarn-over hole. Give the yarn a slight tug, bring the yarn to the back in order to knit, then give the yarn another tug before knitting. The cascading strands are gone, and the buttonhole has been hiked up and reinforced. It almost looks like a vertical slit.

Working into the yarn-over eyelet

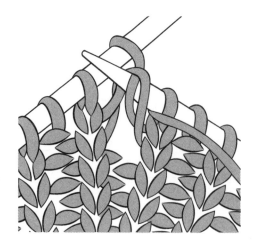

A perfect
buttonhole

Making Buttonholes in a Garter Stitch Band

You can knit into a yarn-over hole, too.
Working buttonholes on a garter stitch band
is easy because all the stitches are the
same. Work up to any stitch where you
would like a buttonhole and yarn over, knit 2
together. On the wrong side, just knit. On the
following row, when you get to the stitch
above the yarn-over hole, knit into the yarn-
over hole instead by inserting the needle
from front to back, then drop the stitch directly above the yarn-over hole. You also can
work this reinforced buttonhole in seed
stitch or any pattern stitch.

Sewing on Buttons

Sewing on buttons is another of my least favorite things to do. There are two kinds of buttons: ones with holes and ones with shanks. I love shanks, and there are several reasons why they're the only kind I will use. With a flat, or sew-through, button with holes, not only is the thread visible, but the button winds up being too close to the fabric, and as a result the button band can dimple in when you button the button band over it.

To avoid this in the sewing world, instructions suggest using a toothpick or coin below the button before sewing to create a space between the button and the band. After sewing on the button, you create a shank by wrapping the thread around the sewing thread. Too much of a big knotted mess for me.

Creating a
sewn shank

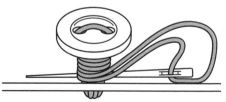

Knitting on Buttons

I have not sewn on a button in more than fifteen years. I knit on my buttons. There are two ways to do it.

USING DENTAL FLOSS. For the first method, you need a shank button and a 4-inch (10cm) piece of dental floss—waxed is best. You will use the floss to thread the stitch through the shank hole of the button. Work up to a stitch

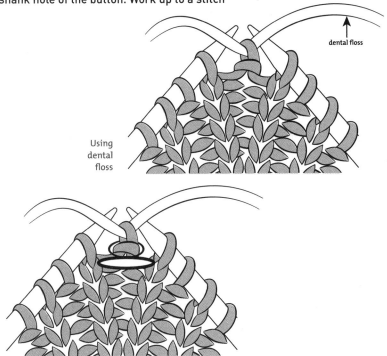

dental floss

Using
dental
floss

where you want the button to be, insert the floss through the next stitch, and take the stitch off the needle. The floss acts as a stitch holder. Line up the floss ends, thread both ends through the button shank hole, and push down on the button until you pull the stitch through the shank hole. Place the stitch back on the left needle, make sure the button is facing the right way, knit the stitch, and then remove the floss.

USING A CROCHET HOOK. For the second method, you need a shank button and a steel crochet hook small enough to go through the hole of the shank. Insert the hook through the shank hole and set it aside. Knit to where you want the button to be, pick up the next stitch with the crochet hook, and pull that stitch through the shank hole. Place the stitch back onto the left-hand needle, make sure the button is facing the right way, and complete the stitch.

The hook method is faster, but the dental floss method may be more convenient because you always have dental floss around. Take a close look at a knitted-on button and you'll see that there are two strands of yarn holding the button firmly in place.

Using a crochet hook

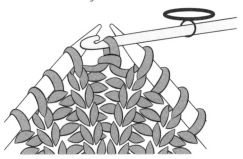

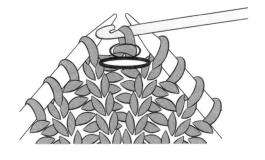

If you plan to knit on buttons, remember the following:

- **No sharp shanks.** The sharp edges will saw at the yarn and eventually break your work.
- **No delicate fibers.** Some yarns, such as angora, almost fall apart when you tug at them.
- **No heavy buttons.** Heavy metal or solid glass will pull too much on the one stitch.
- **No loose gauges.** The button will pull out the stitch and distort the work.
- **Beware the directional button.** That heart may be on its side depending on how it's oriented to the shank and how it sits down over the stitch. That letter U on the button easily can become a C.
- **Use buttons that are washable.**

Lastly, make sure you don't change your mind. If you want to replace the buttons, it means you have to rip out your work, or snip stitches, which requires a different repair job.

Just as you can knit buttons directly onto your work, so too can you apply beads. That means not having to prestring the beads onto the yarn ahead of time. What a boon! In fact, I devote a couple of chapters to this method in my book *Knit and Crochet with Beads*. Check it out.

Weaving in Ends

The key to weaving in ends is to take many
U-turns in your path. A straight line, such as
the simple running stitch, will come out easily. Try to change direction as often as possible, up and down, left and right. Take a look
at the proposed directions that the yarn end
can take in this swatch.

The tool of choice for most of us is the
darning needle. I adore the bent-tipped
Chibi brand from the Japanese toolmaker
Clover. The bent tip really allows you to dig
deep into the little nooks and crannies.

Path for weaving
in yarn ends

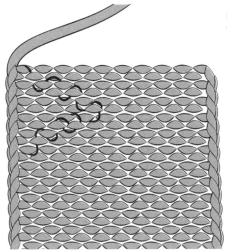

● **TIP** WORKING WITH SHORT ENDS

Most of my ends are not longer than about 2 inches (5cm). I just heard a big thud. It's true. The reason I can get away with this is the reversal of directions that I just talked about. Yet how do I maneuver after threading the needle? The trick is to not thread the needle first. Insert an empty darning needle near where the end of the yarn is, weave it in and out through the fabric in a diagonal line, then thread the yarn end into the needle and draw it through.

Using a Latch Hook

When holding a yarn needle to weave in
ends, I use two or three fingers at most. I
like to get a better grip; I'd rather hold
something firmly in my hand with a knife
hold. Using a small crochet hook can snag
the yarn, however. Luckily, I also happen
to be a machine knitter, and machine knitters have really cool tools. One of them is
the latch hook, which looks like the kind
used for latch hook rugs, but it is smaller.
The one I use is double-ended; the smaller
end is meant for thinner yarns and the
larger end for thicker yarns. I find it easier
to handle than a yarn needle.

When the latch is open, it's shaped like a
hook; when the latch is closed, there's no
open hook to catch or snag the fabric. To use
a latch hook, start at the point where you
want the yarn to end up, then work back
toward the yarn tail. You have to move the
stitches behind the hook in order to fully
close the latch over the yarn tail and then
pull the tail through.

Using a
latch hook

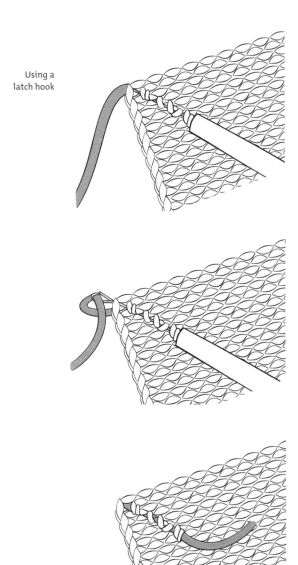

For really slippery ends such as rayon or silk, some knitters have had success keeping the end from raveling by dabbing it with a bit of Fray Check. Before you do that, make sure your yarn is colorfast and that the stuff won't form too hard a ball or bead. Need I say try it out on the swatch first?

● **TIP** BRUSHING MOHAIR OR EYELASH YARN
Just as some fabrics look better with the nap raised, some yarns—such as mohair and eyelash, and sometimes even alpaca, angora, and brushed acrylic—can use some fluffing up from time to time. Some knitted fabrics will tamp down with wear or after washing, and a bit of a touch-up with a brush can infuse new life into these fabrics. If your stitches are uneven or there are some mistakes you want to hide, brushing is great for that, too. You can use a soft metal-bristled brush from a pet supply store. I'm sure the pooch won't mind if you borrow it from time to time.

The Lowdown
from Lily

USE GOOD MATERIALS, needles and yarn that work together and the ones you're most comfortable with so you can **enjoy knitting.**

ALWAYS MAKE A SWATCH. I view swatching much like dating. You want to **try out things** before you commit. I'd rather use up half a ball of yarn and half an hour of my time than to waste fourteen balls of yarn and two months of my time.

ACCEPT YOUR MISTAKES. We knitters are our own worst critics. If someone compliments you on a sweater, don't focus on the mistakes. **Be gentle with yourself,** and accept what you've accomplished.

A LITTLE FORETHOUGHT GOES A LONG WAY. Reel off seaming yarn when casting on for fewer ends to weave in later. Prepare for a left-slanting decrease the row before for a tidier look. Know how many yards of yarn go into a row of your work so you don't run out partway through. Breathe. Taking a breath before you begin and taking your time can be **the best time-saving tactics.**

"GOD IS IN THE DETAILS," said Ludwig Mies van der Rohe, the Bauhaus architect. In knitting, that means evenly space your picked-up stitches as well as buttonholes and buttons **handily and easily**. Mattress seam precisely and you'll have invisible seams. Never bind off too tightly.

IT'S NOT ROCKET SCIENCE. In explaining the logic of how some of my tips have come about, I encourage you to **come up with your own ideas and "aha" moments**. Ironically enough, I taught a class for the Houston knitting guild and, at one point, said, "It's not rocket science." Little did I know that there was a NASA rocket scientist in my class. A shout-out to Gwen W.

Knitting Abbreviations

* *	repeat steps between asterisks as many times as indicated
beg	beginning
BO	bind off
Cbl	cable
CC	contrast color
cn	cable needle
CO	cast on
dpn	double-pointed needle
k	knit
k2tog	knit 2 stitches together (decrease)
kf&b	knit into front and back of same stitch (increase)
LH	left-hand
M1	make 1 stitch (increase)
MC	main color
p	purl
p2tog	purl 2 together (decrease)
pf&b	purl into front and back of same stitch (increase)
pm	place marker
psso	pass slipped stitch over
PU	pick up and knit
rev St st	reverse stockinette stitch
RH	right-hand
RS	right side
skp	slip 1, knit 1, pass slipped stitch over
sl1	slip 1 stitch
sl 1 k	slip 1 stitch knitwise
sl 1 p	slip 1 stitch purlwise
ssk	slip, slip, knit
st(s)	stitch(es)
St st	stockinette stitch
tbl	through the back loop
WS	wrong side
yo	yarn over

Resources

Clover Needlecraft, Inc.
13438 Alondra Blvd.
Cerritos, CA 90703
(562) 282-0200
http://www.clover-usa.com
Chibi darning needles, stitch markers,
light-up crochet hooks, bamboo crochet
hooks, other notions.

Coats and Clark
P.O. Box 12229
Greenville, SC 29612-0229
(800) 648-1479
http://www.coatsandclark.com
Susan Bates crochet tools.

Fiber Fantasy Knitting Products, Ltd.
4876 Butler Rd.
Glyndon, MD 21071
(410) 517-1020
www.woolstock.com
Fiber Fantasy Blockers Kit and Fiber
Fantasy Fold-A-Way Blocking Board.

Fiber Trends
P.O. Box 7266
East Wenatchee, WA 98802
(509) 884-8631
http://www.fibertrends.com/
Needle-felting supplies.

Four Paws
50 Wireless Blvd.
Hauppauge, NY 11788
(631) 434-1100
http://www.fourpaws.com
Pet brushes.

Handler Textile Corp.
60 Metro Way, Dept. #G
Secaucus, NJ 07094
(201) 272-2000
http://goliath.ecnext.com
"Space Board" gridded blocking board.

Knitcraft
215 North Main
Independence, MO 64050
(816) 461-1248
http://www.knitcraft.com
Machine-knitting latch hook.

Knitting Software
1015 Hiland Ave.
Coraopolis, PA 15108
(412) 264-1953
http://www.knittingsoftware.com/
Print-A-Grid.

Prym Consumer USA Inc.
950 Brisack Rd.
Spartanburg, SC 29303-4709
(864) 576-5050
http://www.dritz.com/
Dritz Fray Check.

Wm. Wright Co.
85 South St. P.O.Box 398
West Warren, MA 01092
and Antioch, TN 37013
(877) 597-4448
http://www.wrights.com
Boye crochet hooks.

Bibliography

Chin Lily. *Knit and Crochet with Beads*. Loveland, CO: Interweave Press, 2004.

Kooler Donna. *Encyclopedia of Knitting*. Little Rock, AR: Leisure Arts, 2004.

Square, Vicki. *The Knitter's Companion*. Loveland, CO: Interweave Press, 1996.

Vogue Knitting Magazine Editors. *Vogue Knitting: The Ultimate Knitting Book*. New York: Sixth&Spring Books, 2002.

Acknowledgments

I want to thank Rosy Ngo, who's been ever so patient with me all these years. Of course, there's Melissa Bonventre, not to mention Erica Smith and Betty Wong. Not many people can say that their attorney is also a good friend and fellow knitter/crocheter, but Margo Lynn Hablutzel is all that to me, and more. I'm grateful to Linda Hetzer for listening well and pushing gently and filling in nicely. Most of all, thanks and praise go to technical editor Joan Schrouder. Lastly, I would not be able to do this without the love and support of my long-suffering husband, Cliff. Oh, my computer and scanner and digital camera have been totally indispensable.

Index

A

Abbreviations 202

Adjusting lengths of garments 82–85

Aran yarn 25, 27

Australian yarn 25–26

B

Baby yarn 26

Back stitch 164

Binding off

about:

overview of 56, 148

circular bind-off...154–155

crochet hook bind-off in knit 148–149

crochet hook bind-off in purl...............................150

decrease bind-off 152–153

general guidelines.. 56–57

three-needle bind-off...151

two-needles-and-a-hook bind-off 152

Blocking 65–67, 156–161

Blocking equipment 159–161

Bouclé yarn 22, 23

Bradford worsted system 31

Bread-tie bobbins 94

Brushing fabrics 199

Bulky/super-bulky yarn 26, 27, 61, 72, 73

Buttons

buttonholes for ... 186–189

knitting on 191–194

sewing on 190

spacing evenly 184–185

C

Cable, wrongly crossed 140–144

Casting on.

See also Crocheted cast-on

about: overview of 40

amount of yarn for ..90–96

crochet chain cast-on variation...............105–106

half-hitch cast-on... 41–42

knitted cast-on............. 46

long-tail cast-on.........42–45, 90–96

in pattern 97–98

using mathematics..90–96

Center of ball, finding 86

Chaining on.

See Crocheted cast-on

Chenille yarn 22

Chunky yarn 26

Circular bind-off...154–155

Circular needles

characteristics of......... 14

choosing 16, 17

illustrated 15

joining as you go.. 172–176

joining in round without twisting 107–109

Color

changing mid-row 121

felt-tip marker trick for 144–145

helping read gauge...................... 68–70

stripes (floats) 119–120

Combination knitting ... 130

Conditioning wool yarn 67

Cone yarn

floor lamp set up for 89

removing cone from 89

setting up 88–89

systems of.

See Yarn systems

working with............87–89

Continental metric system 32

Continental style

Eastern knitting and....130

holding needles 38

knitting 93

stitch orientation.....47–48

Cotton 19, 21, 72, 102

Cotton system...........29, 32

Counting rows 133–134

Crocheted cast-on

basic procedure 99–101

chained provisional cast-on 102–104

hook sizes and............101

variation 105–107

Crochet hook bind-off in knit 148–149

Crochet hook bind-off in

purl 150
Crochet hook,
knowing 101
D
Decreases.............125–131
  Eastern or Combination
  knitting and 130
  knit 2 together
  (k2tog) 125
  knit 2 together through
  the back loop
  (k2tog tbl)................... 127
  left-slanting
  decrease 128–129
  slip, knit, pass stitch over
  (skp) 127
  slip, slip, knit (ssk)......126
  throwing opposite way for
  knitting in round and....131
Denier system ...29–30, 32
DK yarn.............. 26, 27, 31
Dropping stitches, to fix
cable......................142–144
Drop-shoulder
sleeves..................178–179
"Dry clean only"
labels..............................66
Duplicate stitch
(Swiss darning) 137–141
  to fix knit to purl 138
  to fix purl to knit..139–140
  to fix wrongly crossed
  cable 140–141
E
Eastern knitting 130

Ends
  connecting. *See* Joining
  short, working with.....196
  weaving in 195–199
English cotton system 32
English, holding..............37
English woolen system ..31
European yarn 25
Eyelash yarn 22, 199
Eyelets
  as buttonholes 186–189
  encoding swatches
  with 63–65
F
Felting
  needle felting..............115
  spit splicing and ..114–115
Fingering weight 26,
  ....27, 32
Finishing. *See also* Binding
off; Seaming
  blocking 156–160
  joining as you go ..172–177
  setting in drop-shoulder
  sleeves 178–179
  weaving in ends ..195–199
Floats....................119–120
French knot 163
G
Garter stitch 52
Garter stitch band,
buttonholes in..............189
Gauge
  after killing fabric........159
  defined 60–62

hung 71–73
  measuring/
  reading 60–62, 67–71
  recommended 25
  swatches 60–65,
  ....67, 68–71
Gauge (for needles) 18
Graph paper, using ..76–79,
  ....82–85, 122–124
H
Half-hitch cast-on 41–42
Hanks of yarn 28–29,
  .... 31–32, 81, 88
Holding needles 36–38
Holding yarn...................38
Hung gauge...............71–73
Increases 132–133
I
Intarsia 121–124
J
Joining
  attaching
  edgings................175–176
  new piece
  on left 174–175
  new piece
  on right...............172–174
  new yarn 112–116
  in round without
  twisting...............107–109
  as you go 172–177
K
"Killing a fabric," ..158–159
Knit 2 together
(k2tog) 125

Knit 2 together through the back loop (k2tog tbl) 127

Knit in back and front...133

Knit in front and back (kf&b) 132–133

Knit stitch 48–49

Knitted cast-on 46

Knit to purl, fixing 138

L

Latch hook, using ..197–199

Lazy purl 130

Left-slanting decrease 128–129

Length of garments, adjusting 82–85

Long-tail cast-on 42–45, 90–96

M

Mattress stitch 167–171

Microfiber yarn 22

Mistakes

accepting 200

dropping stitches to fix.........................142–144

duplicate stitch (Swiss darning) to fix 137–141

felt-tip marker trick to fix 144–145

knit to purl 138

missing color.......144–145

purl to knit..........139–140

wrongly crossed cable...................140–144

N

Needle felting, 115

Needles. *See* also Circular

needles

choosing 16

double-pointed 15

gauge for 18

holding 36–38

matching to yarns .. 32–33

materials 16–17

metric conversion chart...............................17

sizes 17–18

sizing unknown-sized ...18

smoothing out 39

straight....................14, 15

types of....................14–16

Numbering systems (e.g. 2/28). *See* Yarn systems

O

Orientation of stitches....................47–48

P

Picking up stitches ....100–101, 172, 173, 176, ...180–183

Pictures (intarsia) ..121–124

Planning ahead.............201

Purl stitch 50–51, 95–96

Purl to knit, fixing..139–140

R

Resources.....................203

Reverse stockinette stitch 53

Ribbing, 54–55

Ribbon yarn ....22, ...23, 117–118

Round, knitting in. *See* also

Circular references

joining in round without twisting 107–109

throwing opposite way for.........................131

Rows

keeping track of...133–134

single, measuring yarn for.......................113–114

Russian join.................116

S

Scarf or stole yarn requirements 75–76

Seam-as-you-go-cardigan 177

Seaming 162–171

See also Joining

about: overview of 162

back stitch for 164

bread-tie bobbins for yarn 94

ending with French knot 163

mattress stitch for 167–171

single crochet stitch for 166

slip stitch for...............165

starting with slip knot ..162

stripes.................168–171

whipstitch for.............163

yarn requirements for...........................93–94

Seed stitch.....................55

Shoulder, sloping, 135–136

Single crochet stitch.....166

Sleeves, drop-shoulder 178–179

Slingshot formation 42–44, 92

Slip, knit, pass stitch over (skp).............................127

Slip knots.................41, 162

Slip, slip, knit (ssk).......126

Slip stitch 165

Sloping shoulders..135–136

Slubs, nubby, thick and thin yarn 22

Smoothing out tools 39

Sock yarn.........................26

Spit splicing...........114–115

Sport weight yarn.....26, 27, ...28, 32

Stitches. *See also* Decreases; Seaming
  dictionary recommendation...........56
  garter stitch..................52
  joining new yarn...112–116
  knit stitch.................48–49
  orientation of 47–48
  patterns of 52–54
  purl stitch 50–51, 95–96
  reverse stockinette stitch..............................53
  ribbing.....................54–55
  seed stitch 55
  stockinette (jersey) stitch 52–53

Stockinette (jersey) stitch 52–53

Stripes ...119–120, 168–171

Swatches
  encoding 63–65
  gauge 60–65, 67, 68–71
  hung gauge............. 71–73
  measuring 67
  using........................80–81
  value of 60, 65–66, 200
  washing and blocking 65–67, 87–88, 158
  weighing 75–76
  yarn requirements from..........................75–79

Sweaters
  adjusting lengths of.............................82–85
  seam-as-you-go-cardigan 177
  setting in drop-shoulder sleeves.................178–179
  sloping shoulders 135–136
  yarn requirements 76–79

Swiss darning. *See* Dupli cate stitch (Swiss darning)

T

Tex system 31, 32

Three-needle bind-off ..151

Thumb loops 45, 92

Tracking rows 133–134

Two-needles-and-a-hook bind-off 152

W

Weaving in ends....195–199

Weighing swatches...75–76

Whipstitch 163

Wool 19, 20, 27, 67, 158

Worsted system ..28–29, 31

Worsted yarn ....26, ...27, 31, 32

Wraps per inch 26

Y

Yarn(s)
  Australian 25–26
  European, ...25
  fibers 19–21
  finding center of ball of 86
  fuzziness of 22, 23
  hanks of ....28–29, ...31–32, 81, 88
  holding 38
  joining new 112–116
  matching needles to 32–33
  measuring for one row................113–114
  requirements, from swatches.................75–79
  running short and purling on 95–96
  textures...................22–23
  thickness.................23–25
  wraps per inch 26–27

Yarn systems 27–32
  cotton system..........29, 32

Denier system 29–30, 32
  tex system 31, 32
  worsted system...28–29, 31